English Towns in Transition 1500–1700

PETER CLARK and PAUL SLACK

English Towns in Transition 1500–1700

OXFORD UNIVERSITY PRESS

LONDON   OXFORD   NEW YORK

1976

301.363
C

Oxford University Press, Ely House, London W.1.

GLASGOW NEW YORK TORONTO MELBOURNE WELLINGTON
CAPE TOWN IBADAN NAIROBI DAR ES SALAAM LUSAKA ADDIS ABABA
DELHI BOMBAY CALCUTTA MADRAS KARACHI LAHORE DACCA
KUALA LUMPUR SINGAPORE HONG KONG TOKYO

Paperback   ISBN 0 19 28 9060 3
Casebound   ISBN 0 19 21 5816 3

First published in the Oxford Paperbacks University Series 1976
and simultaneously in a cloth bound edition.

Set in Great Britain by Gloucester Typesetting Co. Ltd.
Printed by Fletcher & Son Ltd, Norwich

Contents

List of Maps

Preface

SOME of the arguments presented here were initially aired in the introductory chapter of *Crisis and Order in English Towns 1500–1700*, which was published in 1972. Further detailed research both by ourselves and other urban historians has enabled us to refine and amplify many of the views expounded there. We have also tried to cover some of the questions which for reasons of space we were able only to touch upon on that occasion, in particular the nature of the changes within the urban hierarchy during the sixteenth and seventeenth centuries. At the same time, the format of the present series has meant that we have had to dispense with a heavy scholarly apparatus. Some readers may find it useful to turn to the earlier piece for fuller documentation of specific points.

Urban history is still, we are happy to say, both a friendly and a lively discipline, and our book has benefited immeasurably from many informal discussions with fellow toilers in the field. In particular we are grateful to Drs. John Chartres, Christopher Moxon, John Patten, and William Petchey for their generosity in permitting us to read and make use of their doctoral theses. We are also indebted to Mr. Keith Thomas for his editorial advice and encouragement, Mr. Ronald Turner for drawing the maps on pp. 161–2, the Essex Record Office for permission to reproduce John Walker's map of Chelmsford, and to Routledge and Kegan Paul for permission to reproduce the John Speed map of Southampton. Last but far from least, our thanks are once again due to our respective wives, who have tolerated and even (up to a point) encouraged yet another excursion into the English town and its problematical past.

I

Introduction

BETWEEN 1500 and 1700 England was still very much a rural nation. At least three-quarters of its population, probably more, lived in the countryside and the vast majority of them were employed in agriculture. The political élite comprised the *country* gentlemen and the *landed* aristocracy. The conventional ideals of the society were largely rural ones: husbandmen and yeomen were the only occupational groups unambiguously admired by the government; 'hospitality' in the hamlet and village was the duty of the upper classes, 'charity' towards familiar neighbours in small communities that of others. Yet having said this, there can be little question that towns were of major and growing significance. They were political and religious centres, meeting places for courts, Parliament, justices of the peace, and bishops. They were foci of economic life where agricultural produce was bought and sold. If rural industry was increasingly important, nevertheless its raw materials were bought in the town, its products finished and sold there. Towns were also the social and cultural centres of the country. They housed doctors, lawyers, schools, universities, theatres, and shops; and it was in towns that rents and other landed income were spent. Towns were the essential cogs in the machinery of rural society, providing organization, articulation, and diversity.

There was a great variety of towns in this period. The seven hundred places which could be given the title ranged from metropolitan London with 60,000 people in the 1520s to little market-towns like Banbury, Bideford, and Sutton Coldfield with six or seven hundred. All had their own particular characteristics, vexing and defying the historian who tries to generalize about their character and development. Nor is this the only problem facing the student of the early modern town: others stem from the uneven attention which has been given to different kinds of urban community. Despite recent advances in urban history, most work on the English pre-industrial town has concentrated on the larger and more famous provincial and country towns to the relative neglect of the smaller market centres and even of London itself. Moreover, much of the work has served to underline the individuality and diverse development of different places. We are constantly reminded of the dictum of one of the founders of English urban history, F. W. Maitland: 'There can hardly be a history of the English borough, for each borough has its own history.' In the following pages we have sought both to illustrate the variety of experience of English towns in the early modern period and to outline some of the features and developments which they had in common.

At the outset we are confronted by a problem of definition: what do we understand by a 'town'? What were its essential features? A great mass of literature from urban sociologists and geographers has endeavoured to answer these questions with respect to modern industrial towns. The Chicago school, led by Robert E. Park and his successors, developed an ecological theory of the city, stressing the decisive significance of the urban environment, of population density, communication networks, and residential patterns. This approach gave rise to an important article by Louis Wirth on 'Urbanism as a Way of Life' which added the concept of 'heterogeneity'. By this he meant the diversity of origins, attitudes, and occupations of men in towns which produced distinctive— essentially competitive—social relations and hence distinctive economic, governmental, and class structures. For Wirth a town could be defined as 'a relatively large, dense and permanent settlement of socially heterogeneous individuals'. Such a definition would fit most places which historians recognize as towns, but many of the conclusions and implications which Wirth drew from it, like those of other urban sociologists, are hardly applicable to pre-industrial urban communities.

Some of these discrepancies are noted in the only major work which has so far attempted to theorize about pre-industrial towns, G. Sjoberg's *The Preindustrial City*. He stresses, for example, that far from producing, as Wirth argued, weak links and impersonal relations between co-residents, non-industrial towns often contained closely-knit and interrelated élites with extended families; that far from having a weak class structure, they often had a clearly and rigidly defined one; that they had regulated economic structures in which commercial or industrial activities were often of low status; that communication was often inefficient and took traditional forms; and that the division of labour, far from developing rapidly, was still by product rather than by process. Not all of Sjoberg's implied distinctions between industrial and pre-industrial towns have equal force and validity. The apparent rigid class divisions in many historic towns, for example, may simply have been a reaction to rapid social mobility, mechanisms by which the *nouveaux riches* tried to establish their new status. As Sjoberg himself allows: 'Even where movement of individuals is considerable, personal attributes sharply set pre-industrial urbanites off from one another, giving the actor an *impression* of fixity and marked distance between classes' (our italics). Emrys Jones has pointed out that Sjoberg's work also shares with other writings on the 'pre-industrial town' the tendency to use the term as a residual category into which many different sorts of town from the ancient world to medieval Europe and modern Africa are bundled. Very often the differences between these urban centres are greater than the similarities. Certainly, several of the more important generalizations which Sjoberg makes do not apply to English towns in the early modern period. This is clearly the case with his emphasis on the 'urban character' of the ruling élites in pre-industrial societies, for example. Nevertheless, the book is important: first, because it establishes that the industrial town should not be taken as an urban 'norm'; and secondly, because, like Max Weber's comparable work on classical and medieval towns, it shows the fundamental importance to urban identities of such variables as demography, class, education, and religion, which have sometimes been regarded as merely secondary features.

Similar points could be made about other modern contributions to urban theory. Geographers have stressed the significance of the relationship of the town to its region, and of the relative sizes ('ranking') of towns in a country. Though sometimes losing touch with reality in its mathematical elaboration, their work is of obvious relevance to the marketing functions of early modern English towns and to the overwhelming dominance of London, as a 'primate city'. Social anthropologists have begun to investigate urbanization in developing countries and their examination of such topics as migration, family, and social class sheds light on aspects of urban structure and change in the sixteenth and seventeenth centuries. Historians have likewise ventured to generalize about towns, sometimes stressing the vital defining significance of legal institutions, as in Maitland's work on boroughs, or that of merchants and commerce, as with Pirenne: today both aspects are regarded as important but neither exclusively so. More recently, Fernand Braudel has divided West European towns into 'open', 'closed', and 'subject' categories: the first blending into their hinterlands; the second closed in on themselves and containing an individual way of life; the third closely controlled by princes and states. Braudel's distinctions highlight the significance of the political identity of towns, but leave ample room for argument about the label to be applied to any particular example.

All these contributions have something to offer the student of early modern English towns. Yet they are more helpful in posing questions for investigation—about urban attitudes, structures, behaviour patterns, and so on—than in prescribing simple rules for the identification and classification of towns. One needs to begin with simpler criteria, grounded in distinctions of size and function, but not ignoring other aspects of urban life. We suggest, therefore, that there were five basic and readily recognizable characteristics of English pre-industrial towns: first, an unusual concentration of population; second, a specialist economic function; third, a complex social structure; fourth, a sophisticated political order; and fifth, a distinctive influence beyond their immediate boundaries.

The first two features were necessary to the existence of any town. It is impossible to set any precise lower limit to the size of a town, to quantify the point when it ceases to be a village. When Gregory King listed the relative sizes of English towns in 1696 he included places with between 150 and 200 houses, implying populations sometimes as low as 600, and this was often the size of the smaller market-town. But not all settlements of 600 people were towns, for many did not have a specialized economic function in their neighbourhood. It is this economic function, whether as a market, service, or industrial centre, which is often taken as the simplest criterion for a town. Its necessary concomitant was the employment of a significant, if variable, section of its population in non-agricultural occupations. At the same time, as we shall see in later chapters, the special economic role of a town was expressed in the diversity of occupations which it contained. The larger the town, the greater the diversity. Whereas the sixteenth-century provincial capital of Norwich had well over one hundred different trades, most market-towns made do with between twenty and thirty.

The other fundamental characteristics distinguishing urban from rural communities were common to the majority of towns, although they were not shared by some of the smaller centres. As we shall see in chapter eight, the English town in this period was characterized by a more overtly stratified social pyramid than was to be found in the countryside. There were sharp differences both of wealth and status, the latter underlined by much of the institutional fabric of town life. Paradoxically, urban élites probably experienced a greater turnover of personnel than their village counterparts, though this may have reflected high levels of migration rather than rapid social mobility within towns. Once again the larger the town the more complicated its social order. This was also the case with political organization. Throughout the Middle

Ages towns had fought to secure political privileges: from grants of markets; or freedom from tolls and the jurisdiction of manorial and hundredal courts; to chartered status as boroughs—some able to send representatives to Parliament. By the later fifteenth century formal incorporation, recognizing the right of the community to act collectively, had become the acknowledged summit of a town's ambition. Along with these achievements went the development of councils and courts, municipal officials and gilds to regulate the political and economic life of the urban community. By 1500 most towns enjoyed some privileges of this kind; only the smaller centres were still ruled by a lord through his manorial court. So far as the extra-urban impact of towns is concerned, this was mainly a feature of the developed towns, the cathedral cities, and county towns. By the end of the Middle Ages their churches and schools, their plays and processions, along with the consumer habits of their citizens, all proclaimed the identity of the town and influenced the countryside around it.

These five elements in our urban definition are inevitably rather rough tools for social analysis. But it is reassuring to find them reflected in contemporary views of the town, imprecise though these were. True, the term 'town' might refer to any settlement from the village upwards, but for Gregory King and earlier observers 'cities and market-towns' were clearly distinguished by their size from the rest. For John Hooker, the Elizabethan historian of Exeter, as for some modern sociologists, urban size and population density also imposed political demands and social constraints, although he was optimistically vague about them: he defined a *civitas* as a 'multitude of people assembled and collected to the end to continue and live together in a common society yielding dutiful obedience unto their superiors and mutual love to [one] another'. Thomas Wilson, writing in 1600, thought first of the wider influence of towns, putting at the top of his list the twenty-six cities which were the seats of bishops and the 289 towns 'not inferior in greatness . . . being most walled towns' and shire towns; he also stressed their political autonomy, every one 'being, as it were, a Common

Wealth among themselves'. The author of a 'Discourse of Corporations' in the 1580s emphasized their economic function: 'it is the site and place where every town or city is builded which is the chief cause of the flourishing of the same, or else some special trade and traffic appropriate to the same, and not the incorporation thereof.' And Robert Brady, writing *An Historical Treatise of Cities and Burghs* at the very end of our period, was as impressed as later historians by the difficulty of distinguishing precisely between market-towns and boroughs with more sophisticated political structures: the former might not have 'burgh liberties and royalties, free burgesses, a merchant gild, or community and peculiar officers, which were the characteristics of a burgh', he wrote, but 'by outward appearance in many things [they] could not be distinguished' from them. All this would suggest that our five defining criteria for urban communities will not lead us far astray.

How many towns were there then in Tudor and Stuart England? Our ignorance about the fate of some of the smaller settlements which had market rights makes it impossible to answer this question with any certainty. But a maximum figure of 700 would not be a gross exaggeration. The great age for the founding of English towns was in the two centuries before 1350, by which time 2,000 settlements had been granted markets: 600 of these were also boroughs. In the century of population decline after the Black Death, however, many markets disappeared and some of the 609 boroughs which still existed in 1500 had probably faded into insignificance: Professor Everitt estimates that by the beginning of Elizabeth's reign there were less than 750 market-towns, many of them, of course, without borough charters. Even so England may still have been over-supplied with towns. In the course of the sixteenth and seventeenth centuries there were various newcomers, but other centres decayed and their markets were discontinued. As we shall see, the main developments of our period took the form of changes in the fortunes and relative importance of established towns rather than major additions to, or subtractions from, the stock of urban settlements. However, the decline of some smaller market centres in the later seventeenth century is likely to have pushed the total number of towns slightly downwards, even allowing for the arrival of numerous new spa and industrial centres at the end of our period. Thomas Wilson thought that there were 666 cities and market-towns in 1600, and although Gregory King and John Adams produced figures of 795 and 780 towns at the end of the century, contemporary hearth tax assessments show that some of these settlements had only a few dozen inhabitants. Dr. Chalklin believes that in 1700 there were about 600 towns with populations of more than four to five hundred.

These six or seven hundred towns were unevenly distributed over the countryside. There was a greater concentration in the lowland zone of the south and east than elsewhere. In the later Middle Ages there had been some tilting of the balance towards the south-west, with the rise of the textile industries in the western counties and the growth of towns like Exeter and Totnes. There was also some redistribution towards the North and the West Midlands in the seventeenth century, based again partly on industrial changes and the rise of Birmingham and the Lancashire and West Riding towns. (This latter development is to some extent reflected in our maps of the major English towns in 1520 and 1700.) But the urban predominance of lowland England, associated as it was with the national distribution both of wealth and population, remained marked throughout our period.

Using our five-fold definition of a town we can range these urban settlements, according to their functions and characteristics, in a hierarchy stretching from London at the top down to the smallest market centre. This urban hierarchy contained three broad categories of town. At the lowest level was the most numerous group, between five and six hundred towns, exhibiting three and sometimes only two of the characteristics we have listed: population density, economic specialization and often, but not always, distinctive social and political structures. In 1500 they included lesser market centres like Wotton-under-Edge in Gloucestershire and Lutterworth in Leicestershire, along with decaying boroughs like Winchelsea and Stamford with only localized spheres of influence. Their populations were usually small and where, as in the case of Cranbrook in the Weald of Kent, the number of inhabitants may have been quite large, the density of population was probably low. In the second rank of the hierarchy were towns with a wider impact, acting as regional centres with hinterlands which often included smaller market centres. Their populations commonly ranged between 1,500 and 5,000 in 1500, though some of them had numbers approaching 7–8,000 by 1700. Most still had specialized industries in 1500; several were ports; they included the university towns and lesser cathedral cities. But typical of them were the county towns like Northampton and Bury St. Edmunds, social and political centres for the gentry as well as focal points for local economies. There were probably about a hundred of these towns and by 1700 they were all incorporated. Together with the market centres they formed the rank and file of English country towns in our period.

At the head of the established urban hierarchy were the largest and richest towns, dominating whole regions of England and providing services which no other town could rival. There were six or seven besides London. They certainly included York, Bristol, Norwich, Exeter, and Newcastle, which had populations over 7,000 in 1500 and over 11,000 in 1700. At the start of the sixteenth century Coventry and Salisbury probably had some claim to inclusion, while Colchester and Yarmouth were both towns of more than 10,000 people by 1700, although they did not have the regional impact of the other centres. London, however, exceeded all these in size and importance and could claim a category of its own. The growth of its population alone, from 60,000 at the beginning of our period to more than 500,000 by its end, made it the most striking urban phenomenon in Western Europe, rivalled only by the rise of Amsterdam. All other English towns were dwarfed by comparison. As early as 1543 London paid as much in the subsidy as all the provincial towns put together. With its consumers influencing local economies throughout most of southern England, its merchants increasingly dominating English trade, and its fashions and culture dictating provincial norms, it exemplifies most clearly the enormous hold which capital cities were able to exert over centralized states in the Europe of the *ancien régime*.

By 1700 the overall picture of English urban society was also complicated by the appearance of a range of new towns —industrial towns like Halifax and Manchester, dockyard towns like Chatham and Portsmouth, and the spas such as Bath and Tunbridge Wells. Though some were little more than villages at the start of our period, the late seventeenth century saw them develop as a distinct urban phenomenon in their own right. In chapter three we shall see how their orientation was often markedly different from that of more traditional centres. Above all, they were distinguished by a single highly specialized economic role, often associated with rapid population growth. At the same time their political structures and cultural functions were usually simple and undeveloped. In the early eighteenth century the new towns even began to form their own urban hierarchy parallel to, and in rivalry with, the established ranking we have just described. At its head was an array of major industrial centres in the North and Midlands, including Manchester, Leeds, and Birmingham. But for most of our period the new towns were still only beginning to make their presence felt.

There was thus a wide variety of urban types in early modern England, and we shall discuss some of their individual characteristics in chapters two to five. But one feature of this classification deserves comment. Compared with other countries in Western Europe even England's varied urban hierarchy lacked an important element—an adequate complement of major provincial towns. In the early seventeenth century, forty-two European towns had populations of more than 40,000: six of them were in France, seven in Spain, and seven even in the much smaller area of the Netherlands. England had only London. As a result, urban England appears at first sight to be a world of small market-towns and boroughs with populations of less than 2,000. These certainly formed the vast majority of English towns. But if we count heads, rather than towns, a more balanced picture emerges. Even including in our calculation the smallest market-towns counted by Gregory King, by 1700 more than half of all town

dwellers were probably living in communities with populations in excess of 5,000, one-third of the total in London. We
do not have the data to make similar estimates for 1500, but
it is likely that at least a third of urban residents were then in
towns of more than 2,500 people. The experience of urban
life in a large and crowded town was, therefore, already
relatively common in 1500 and became much more so during
the next two centuries. The number of large towns in England
might be small but they determined the lives of a high
proportion of the urban population of the country.

All this, however, begs the vital question: what proportion
of the total population of England lived in towns between
1500 and 1700? Once again most of our evidence is confined
to the later seventeenth century. Taking together all the 795
cities and market-towns of Gregory King and accepting his
estimates of their size, we find that they contained roughly
25 per cent of the total English population; and if we exclude
towns with less than 200 houses (or $c.$ 1,000 inhabitants) to
avoid doubtful cases, the proportion was about 20 per cent.
This was probably a relatively high degree of urbanization
compared with most other European countries. The urban
populations of France and of Lower Austria, for example,
have been estimated at 16 per cent and 17 per cent in the
seventeenth century. Yet even England could not compete
with the urban development of the Dutch Republic: thus in
the province of Holland as many as 59 per cent of the
population lived in towns of more than 3,000 people in 1622.

Unfortunately, we cannot compare King's figures with
similar estimates for early Tudor England, although the
proportion then must have been much smaller. Nonetheless,
we can use the work of recent historians to furnish approxi-
mate figures for the size of the largest towns both in 1520 and
in 1700. Map 1 shows the fifteen English towns with populations of 4,000 or more in 1520; their aggregate populations
formed little more than 6 per cent of the country's total.
There had probably been little change here for more than a
century, since it has been estimated that 5·46 per cent of the
population in 1377 lived in towns with populations over
3,200. By 1700, however, the situation was very different, as

Map 2 suggests. There were then at least thirty towns with populations of 5,000 or more, and together they contained 15 per cent of the country's population. Since the population of England had roughly doubled in the interim, this was a formidable increase. Most of it was due to the expansion of London, raising its population from less than 3 per cent of the total to 10 per cent, but other towns had grown too. There was still only a small minority of the population living in towns in 1700 but compared with the later Middle Ages the two centuries since 1500 had been a period of substantial and sustained urbanization.

Other changes of equal significance will occupy our attention in later chapters. As we shall see, urban growth was not continuous, or as our maps indicate, universal. It is true that the provincial capitals still retained their importance, that some county centres like Leicester and Nottingham had gradually expanded and pushed their way on to the map, and that older towns like Colchester had adapted their industries to fit and flourish in new circumstances. But the spectacular sectors of growth by 1700 were, apart from London, the ports and dockyard towns like Liverpool, Portsmouth, and Chatham, and the new centres of industry like Birmingham, Manchester, and Sunderland. There were casualties as well as beneficiaries too, and they were often the medium-sized corporate towns which had supplied the dominant urban image in the later Middle Ages. Even towns like Salisbury and Coventry which retained large populations in 1700, had lost their fifteenth-century prosperity and provincial capitals like Bristol and Norwich which had new roles by 1700, had faced decline in the early and middle decades of the sixteenth century. In fact by the 1540s, as the author of the *Discourse of the Commonweal* remarked, decay afflicted 'the most part of all the towns of England, London excepted'.

Our still partial knowledge of the late medieval town makes it impossible to date with any accuracy the origins of these critical circumstances. Certainly many towns had begun to contract before 1500. But the largest of them had for long avoided the worst potential consequences of falling populations after the Black Death. Indeed, the early fifteenth century was a golden age for towns like Salisbury, Southampton, and Bristol and a comparison of the subsidy assessments of 1334 and 1514–15 does not suggest that the urban sector in general had suffered any greater reduction in prosperity than the country as a whole in the later Middle Ages; it may even have increased its share of the nation's wealth. What is clear is that by the middle of the sixteenth century urban decay was widespread and affected most aspects of town life, and that recovery was often slow and never certain.

Basic to the critical difficulties faced by English towns in our period was the vulnerability of urban communities to forces outside their control. Towns were not their own masters in early modern England and they were less so at the end of our period than at the beginning. Possibly the maintenance and certainly the growth of their populations depended on immigration from outside and hence on demographic surpluses in the countryside. Their function as markets and distributive centres was based on agricultural specialization and consumer demand in their hinterlands. Politically, towns were dependent on royal favour for their privileges and on the patronage of the nobility and gentry for influence at Court, and they increasingly suffered both royal and gentry involvement in their affairs. Although they were not, as Thomas Wilson pointed out, ruled by royal governors like the Spanish *corregidores*, they were far from enjoying the autonomy of many Italian, German, or Dutch cities. Even their cultural independence was attenuated as their civic and religious ceremonies and institutions withered at the Reformation, and by 1700 the gentry progressively dictated the social diversions and intellectual life of towns. All in all, it seems evident that for most of our period the initiative and the balance of advantage in the close interrelationship between town and country did not lie with the towns.

This interdependence of town and country should not be taken to imply that there were no obvious boundaries between them or that there was not a specifically 'urban' quality of life, distinct from that of the countryside, in early modern England. As we shall see, the countryside in many ways permeated even the largest towns, with their gardens and fields. But the walls, churches, and market-places of the medium-sized and larger towns gave them a distinct physical image just as their political institutions separated them from the manors and hundreds around them. Urban habits of dress and diet were more varied and commonly thought to be more wasteful and luxurious. The density of urban populations also brought characteristics which modern urban sociologists would recognize. There was more 'heterogeneity' than in the village, since town populations were usually recruited from widely diverse origins and occupied many different trades. There were also socially segregated, residential patterns, though the rich lived in the heart of towns not on the periphery, and place of work and place of residence were not yet separated. Again, geographical and social mobility were more pronounced in towns.

Whether the relative impersonality of urban life had damaging social effects comparable to those listed by urban sociologists is still unclear. It was mitigated to some degree by trade, gild, and parish organizations which helped to lessen the casual nature of many urban relationships. It is possible that kinship ties may have become more, rather than less, important for migrants to towns; such ties certainly played a part in defining their movements. But we can probably say that near relatives were less likely to live close to one another in urban than rural society. At the same time, *pace* Sjoberg, there were no extended families in these towns any more than in the English countryside. There were, on the other hand, unusually large households in the more prosperous urban parishes, providing a 'family' for apprentices and servants, while at the other extreme lodgers and single- and two-person households were common in poorer parts of towns. But the history of the English urban family has still to be written. We have little more information about other modern indicators of the quality of urban life. There is, as yet, no evidence that suicide and illegitimacy rates were significantly higher in towns, although the incidence of theft and literacy was probably enhanced as a result of increased urban opportunities for both.

The rhythms of urban occupations separated from the countryside must have demanded different habits and attitudes of mind. The discipline of regular work was one example: a fifteenth-century writer succinctly noted that 'in cities and towns men rule them by the clock'. Religious attitudes may also have been different where economic life was regulated less by the weather than by individual enterprise. A Jacobean preacher thought that 'the frequency of sermons seems most necessary in cities and great towns, that their inhabitants who . . . see for the most part but the works of men, may daily hear God speaking unto them.' Certainly organized religion had a weaker hold and religious dissidence a greater opportunity in towns than in the countryside. But these remain dark areas of urban history. Recent work warns us against exaggerating either the rationality and anonymity of the town or the conservatism and social equilibrium of the village.

Nevertheless, urban life was decisively influenced by problems which rural society experienced only to a far lesser degree. The need to provide food, water, and rudimentary public hygiene for dense populations; the problems of public order presented by the sharp contrast between rich and poor; the high mortality rates and rapid turnover of population; the devastating crises of plague and fire: all created acute pressures within urban society, sometimes resulting in distinctive urban institutions and regulations. In particular the immigration of the rural poor and dislocations in urban industries made poverty a permanent and escalating burden for early modern towns, taxing their financial, administrative, and political resources to the limit. For most of our period it was severe stresses such as these rather than any more positive attainments which served to separate town from countryside.

There can be little question that between 1500 and 1700 English urban society was affected by important, often radical changes. As Robert Jenison of Newcastle declared in *The Cities Safetie* (1630): there was here no 'abiding city, . . . considering all things now are so uncertain'. It is true that there was still considerable continuity in town life as we shall see in the following pages. It is also evident that there was no uniform pattern of stress encompassing all the towns of the kingdom at one time: there was a multitude of local variations. Nonetheless, one can isolate and identify critical developments in at least two main areas. First there was conflict and tension within the urban hierarchy, affecting the relations between market-town and county town, county town and provincial capital, provincial capital and the metropolis. This theme, with the complicating factor of the rise of the new towns, will be discussed in chapters two to five. The second main area of crisis and change related to the various specific features and functions of urban society in this period, demographic, economic, and the like. These will be considered in the last half of the book.

Country Towns

WE can conveniently begin our consideration of the different sorts of town in the urban hierarchy by examining the country towns, those small and medium-sized communities which formed the vast majority of urban settlements in early modern England. As we have seen, they covered a wide spectrum. At the bottom were the ubiquitous market-towns, with populations sometimes as low as 600; at the top were about 100 county centres, almost all of them chartered boroughs, the largest with populations of 5,000 or so in 1500. The two categories were not rigidly separated from one another. For in between were various urban hybrids, decayed and declining boroughs on the one hand, and a few prosperous market centres acquiring new functions and breaking out from their market-town role on the other. But the two groups had different characteristics and we shall consider each in turn, starting with the simpler market-towns.

In the early sixteenth century there were more than 500 of them. The next two hundred years saw a variety of smaller centres like Tutbury in Staffordshire and Thornbury in Gloucestershire lose their rudimentary urban status, though this numerical decline was to some extent offset by an accession of new towns, including Aynho in Northampton-shire, Stevenage in Hertfordshire, and Hawkshead in Lancashire. So far as their origin is concerned, there were probably three main types of market-town: the wholly new or 'planted' towns founded in the two or three centuries after the Norman Conquest, including Market Harborough and Stony Stratford; the 'organic' towns such as Ashford and

Lutterworth which developed from larger villages between the eleventh and fourteenth centuries; and 'primary' centres like Wye, Melton Mowbray, and Charlbury whose settlement may be dated much earlier, perhaps in the sub-Roman period.

Not surprisingly, the location of a market-town reflected a wide range of variables, among them the suitability of the site, the presence of good communication routes by road and river, and seigneurial interest in securing a market grant from the Crown. Most important, however, was the need for a prosperous, or at least a developing, rural hinterland which would use the market centre as its prime outlet. The national topography of market-towns was itself an index of the regional variations in the agrarian economy. The highest density of market centres in the sixteenth century was in the south, particularly in the Home Counties, with their thriving cultivation of cereals and other arable produce. Further north, in Yorkshire and Cumberland, the mainly pastoral economy and lower population levels required a much thinner scattering of market-towns. There were also quite marked sub-regional differences. In Lancashire, for instance, the two upland areas of Rossendale and Bowland Fells had few urban outlets, most of their limited trade being handled by towns on their flanks. By contrast the more intensive arable farming in the peat-free lowlands and the Ribble Valley sustained a network of relatively busy market centres.

Agriculture pervaded the life of the market-town. Its central institution was the market square which in many places had determined the lay-out of the rest of the town. At Thame the great cattle market occupied a wide oblong area in the midst of the community and shops and houses spread out around it. The countryside intruded in other ways as well. The two or three principal streets of the market-town were frequently a rambling mixture of houses, workshops, orchards, and garden plots. Lacking the walls of the larger urban centres, the market-town had its houses, even on the main street, backing onto the fields of the neighbouring countryside—as one can see from a map of Chelmsford in 1591 (fig. 1). In some towns a significant number of the inhabitants engaged directly in farming. Though this was apparently less common in the West Midlands than elsewhere, at Minchinhampton and Painswick in Gloucestershire the proportions of the population engaged in agriculture in 1608 were as high as 22 and 37 per cent. In addition, traders and craftsmen frequently kept up husbandry as a by-employment. At Ashby de la Zouch virtually everyone had some stake in agriculture.

Yet despite these strong rural overtones there were important differences between the market-town and the village. One obvious distinction was the existence of a market. Yet this was not entirely conclusive, for while every market-town had a market, not all market centres were fully-fledged towns: some were simply villages which came to urban life once a week on market-day. Other variables have then to be taken into account. Population was clearly important. Gregory King wrote in the 1690s of small towns with as few as 150 households or roughly 600 inhabitants; but that was at a time of stagnation for many market-towns. Earlier in the century the majority of market centres probably had at least 900 townsfolk. North Walsham had about 900, Ashby approximately 1,200, Cranbrook nearer 2,000. This was in contrast to an average village population of less than 200.

The typical market-town also provided an array of economic services which could not be found in the village. Once or twice a week the market itself served as an exchange centre for a rural area whose radius, in Lancashire for instance, extended up to seven miles. By the seventeenth century there was a growing tendency for larger markets to specialize in particular commodities, caps at Bewdley, stockings at Evesham, eels at Langport. But most small towns still relied on general, miscellaneous markets. In addition, market-towns usually possessed annual or six-monthly fairs which attracted vendors from a greater distance, though the catchment area varied considerably from region to region. However, fairs were never a purely urban phenomenon: in Kent over half the fairs were held outside towns, often in small villages.

This marketing function of the small country town also

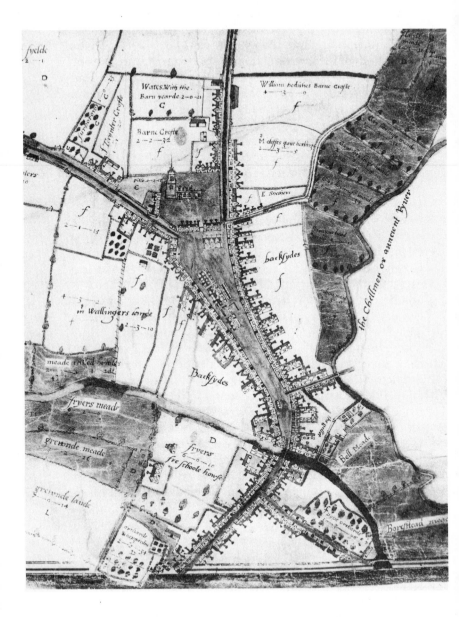

bred a variety of crafts and other semi-specialist occupations. In the early Tudor period market centres like Ashford and Sittingbourne in East Kent included drapers, weavers, smiths, tailors, and wax-chandlers among their townsmen, and East Anglian market-towns often had more than twenty recorded occupations. With the rapid expansion of internal trade during the period, the bustle of farmers and traders produced a host of victuallers, innkeepers, and alehouse-keepers. Ashby was said to have more than forty tippling houses in 1627. In the late seventeenth century the more substantial victualling houses took a growing share of whole-sale trade away from the open market. The latter also began to lose out to the inns and alehouses in the retail trade, so that by 1700 retailers were using inns as temporary shops, thereby foreshadowing the late eighteenth-century appearance of permanent shops in most provincial towns.

The social organization of the market-town had a good deal in common with rural society. Social attitudes were determined by face-to-face relationships and there was little of the impersonal secondary contact which was increasingly the norm in the larger cities, especially London. On the other hand, the extremes of the social structure may have been more obvious than in the average rural community. By the 1660s half the inhabitants of the Kentish market-towns of Tonbridge, Ashford, and Cranbrook were too poor to be chargeable to the Hearth Tax. In the previous century there had been a large influx of rural poor into market centres: in 1624, for example, Ashby relieved nearly seventy poor people from outside the town. At the other social extreme, the leading townsmen not only became more wealthy but found ways of displaying their wealth in an increasingly distinctive

Map of Chelmsford drawn by John Walker in 1591, showing how the shape of a small country town was dictated by its market. By 1591 there were already encroachments on the market-place: permanent houses and stalls in a 'Middle Row', and the Sessions House (below the church), probably built in 1569, which was used as a corn market as well as a court. The buildings, according to Walker, were of 'timber and tile', and they show chimneys and upper storeys which had been unusual before 1540. Note the free school at the bottom of the plan in the growing suburb of Moulsham, and the courtyards of the inns on the main street. The 'backsydes' belonged to the houses along the street, as did some of the 'meades' or pieces of meadow along the rivers, emphasizing the integration of town and countryside.

fashion, in their housing, clothes, education, and leisure activities. In this way they copied their betters in the larger urban centres.

The political structure of the market-town also had some rural overtones. Like the village it lacked that peculiar *imprimatur* of the corporate town, the royal charter. In consequence, the political organization of the market-town was usually relatively simple. There was no special magisterial bench, with extensive regulatory powers, and no array of civic courts. Town affairs were under the control of county justices meeting at quarter sessions. Nonetheless, most market-towns had at least some quasi-political institutions, capable of serving as a focus for civic life and as a channel of communication between the townsmen and outsiders. One institution was the manorial court. At Ashford in Kent the manorial court belonged to a leading local landowner, but it also fulfilled an important urban role. Its jury was made up of prominent townsmen, its bye-laws covered a wide range of urban concerns, from poverty to theft, and the steward of the court, a local lawyer, acted as the town's spokesman in commercial disputes with other towns. Elsewhere, however, as at Aylesbury, the lord of the manor was concerned to keep the local court for his own seigneurial ends. In such cases the townsfolk had to fall back on other communal meeting places, such as the parish vestry. Originally an ecclesiastical institution, the parish had by 1600 acquired a number of administrative duties, and these were frequently managed by a caucus of the parish élite. In market-towns, like Cranbrook and Chelmsford, this oligarchic grouping took the lead in general civic business: parish government became town government.

The parish vestry regularly overlapped with another semi-political organ, widespread in market-towns by 1600: the local charitable trust endowed for educational or poor relief purposes. In Leicestershire towns like Market Harborough, for example, school trusts frequently functioned as active sub-corporate institutions. A combination of posts as school trustee and vestryman might give the leading inhabitants of a market-town quite extensive powers: while the vestry offered a limited administrative mechanism, the trust provided both school funds and patronage over school lands and leases.

Schools, in fact, were a distinctive feature of market-towns from the sixteenth century onwards. It is true that by 1600 a significant proportion of rural parishes enjoyed the sporadic services of an elementary schoolmaster. But the educational function of the market-town was much more extensive, with a number of petty schools and frequently an endowed grammar school attracting pupils from a considerable radius. William Lilly, the astrologer, recalled how in 1613 his family of decayed yeomen farmers from Diseworth in North Leicester-shire sent him to Ashby to John Brinsley, the town school-master: a man 'of great abilities for instruction of youth in the Latin and Greek tongues; he was very severe in his life and conversation and did breed up many scholars for the universities'. Tonbridge grammar school similarly prospered under an able line of masters, recruiting pupils from most of the Home Counties. But the educational ambitions of the majority of townsmen and local peasants were limited to the acquisition of basic literacy, enabling them or their children to participate in the growth of internal trade centred on the market-town. For these people the town's petty school was a cheap and increasingly popular means of instruction.

In the late sixteenth and early seventeenth centuries, market-towns were also important centres of evangelical Puritanism. As well as the ordinary church services, extra sermons were given on market-days with a special appeal to peasants thronging the town. Sometimes these sermons were delivered by specially appointed preachers or lecturers. One such man was the Presbyterian John Strowd, whose market-day sermons at Cranbrook made him famous throughout the Weald of Kent, and whose suspension by the Archbishop of Canterbury in 1576 provoked a noisy outcry from landowners and villagers across the countryside, angry that 'our country be deprived of so diligent a labourer in the Lord's harvest'. Market-days might also be the opportunity for more informal discussion between the godly of town and countryside. Richard Condor from Cambridgeshire described how in the 1630s he used to accompany his father to Royston market:

'the custom of the good men in those days was, when they had done their marketing, to meet together and spend their penny together' on a private meal, 'when, without interruption, they might talk freely of the things of God; how they had heard on the Sabbath-day and how they had gone on the week past etc . . .' In the heyday of English Puritanism the market-towns stood in the vanguard of the attack on rural ignorance and Papist superstition.

There were clearly important fluctuations in the fortunes of market-towns during our period. Though some 'primary' centres may have originated much earlier, the great age for the establishment of market centres had been the twelfth and thirteenth centuries, following the Norman Conquest and the rapid expansion of population, agriculture, and trade. There followed a period of contraction, with many of the more marginal centres disappearing as population declined after the Black Death; indeed the number of market-towns never returned to its earlier peak. Nevertheless, the sixteenth and early seventeenth centuries saw a marked resurgence of the market-town. Not only did a number of new centres appear on the map, but the older settlements flourished. There was a good deal of new building and improvement to existing properties; the markets were crowded with stalls, traders, and customers; relatively autonomous political institutions were developing: and culturally the market-town now exercised a very definite educational and religious influence over the adjoining countryside. By the late seventeenth century, however, the situation had changed; market-towns no longer held their position as one of the more buoyant sectors of English urban society. It is true that a number of the larger market centres continued to thrive, like Ashford and Wymondham. But other smaller towns were starting to shrink or stagnate. Thus Ashby was evidently in decline by 1700, a shadow of its earlier, bustling importance, and in western England the number of market-towns actually fell by a quarter in certain counties.

Some of the reasons for the wavering fortunes of the market-town have a general significance for urban society and will be mentioned again in later chapters. Rapid population growth, particularly marked between 1570 and 1620, brought with it an expansion of internal trade which benefited the market-towns: neither factor was so important in the later seventeenth century. The increase in political stability under the Tudors also encouraged trading in the lesser markets, while improvements in transport facilities in the later seventeenth century benefited the larger towns at the expense of the smaller. Not least important, however, was one of the features of market-towns which we have just discussed. The simplicity and flexibility of their institutions undoubtedly gave them a major advantage over most other country towns in the competition for control of internal trade in the sixteenth century. The same lack of sophisticated institutions may well have made them particularly vulnerable after the Restoration to increased seigneurial conservatism in the countryside, hostile to their role as religious and educational centres.

Naturally, not all market-towns fitted into the pattern we have just described. Some, like Birmingham, developed rapidly from undistinguished market status in the 1530s to major industrial communities by 1700. Others, most notably the early 'primary' settlements such as Banbury or Maidstone, graduated during the period into quite important county towns, complete with their own Tudor charters. In the opposite direction moved old corporate towns like Stamford whose medieval greatness was almost totally eclipsed by the sixteenth century, when its population was as low as 800. William Lambarde commented on the almost equally decayed city of Lincoln in 1584 that it was 'little better than . . . a common market town'.

In general, however, most county towns can be identified as belonging to a relatively distinct urban class, separate from the market-towns. During the seventeenth century there were probably around a hundred county towns, with the highest density in the south and west. Sussex, for instance, had two or three county centres, Lewes, Chichester, and possibly Rye, while the Midland counties of Bedfordshire and Leicestershire had to make do with one each.

The variables which determined the location of county

towns were essentially the same as those for market centres, but there were quantitative differences. Most county towns served as the focus for a web of major trade routes, while their hinterland was usually both more extensive and more diverse than that of the market-town: often it embraced or overlapped with the market areas of smaller places. Thus in Lancashire, while the small market centres traded with adjacent villages, the county town of Preston occupied a central marketing position in regard to both the intensive arable farming of central Lancashire, and the pastoral specialization of the North. As H. B. Rodgers has argued, 'no town was better placed to benefit from the trade which inevitably sprang from these regional contrasts, with their associated surpluses and deficits'. This trading strength was buttressed by the town's position at the centre of the county's road network.

Many of the older county towns were also located in places of strategic significance. Lincoln was sited by the Romans on the high promontory of the Lincoln Edge, commanding both the fens and the main trackways into the North; the Normans confirmed this strategic importance by building a large castle in the upper half of the city. Of course it would be wrong to over-emphasize this military factor in the evolution of the medieval town. Nonetheless, many county centres retained a residual, mainly defensive, military role into the later Middle Ages.

Certainly, at the start of the sixteenth century the town wall was still one of the most distinctive features of older county towns like Rye, Lincoln, and Chester. They were always the first aspects noted by Tudor visitors like John Leland, who remarked that 'the town of Canterbury is walled and has five gates'. As well as protecting the citizens, more or less effectively, from the disorders of civil war and rural brigandage, town walls helped the magistracy to control and police the inhabitants and to regulate relations with outsiders, particularly in the field of trade. Not least important, the walls were symbolic, a striking physical testimony to the closed unity of the county town, fortified against the vagaries of the outside world. As such they provided a striking contrast with the openness of the typical market-town.

Having said this, it would be wrong to exaggerate the differences between the market and county town. As in the market-town there were important rural overtones. At Leicester, for example, orchards and gardens were common in the various undeveloped areas within the walls. Similarly, husbandry was a fairly important secondary employment, though less general than in the market centre. Pigs were the most popular livestock and were a notorious source of filth and stench. Cattle were usually kept on the common lands outside the town. At Oxford, Eglentine Browne, a carpenter's wife, was said to have 'two or three milk-beasts which she . . . milks and makes of the milk butter and cheese', presumably for sale in the city markets. Even more important, the occupational structure of the typical county town had a strong bias towards agricultural services. We can see this at Canterbury in the early seventeenth century when as many as 9 per cent of the freemen were engaged in agriculture or agriculture-related trades, making and repairing tools for the East Kent countryside. The close ties between town and country were also underlined by the way in which townsmen often went harvesting in local villages: in 1595 Barnstaple people 'lamented they had lost a fine harvest day' when the Bishop of Exeter came to town.

It is hardly surprising then that the agricultural market was one of the central economic institutions of the county town, just as it was in the smaller centre. Often the county town had a whole series of markets. At Worcester, for instance, English and Welsh cattle were sold in Angel Lane and Dolday respectively, sheep in Broad Street, grain in the Cornmarket, and ironmongery, leather, and woodware in various other parts of the town. At Liverpool all the countrymen selling corn lined up on the main street, those from Lancashire on the east side, those from Cheshire on the west. The normal market radius of the county town was quite extensive—in the case of Worcester about fifteen miles—and this was further enlarged by the importance of twice- or thrice-yearly fairs, often lasting for a week or more. These attracted traders like the pirate London publisher, John Wolfe, who was alleged in 1583 to 'run up or down to all the fairs' in a great part of the realm.

Not only the marketing function but also the occupational structure of the county town was more complex than that of the typical market centre. A recent survey of East Anglian towns has suggested that the larger centres had from forty to one hundred different occupations by the early seventeenth century. In all of them large proportions of the workforce, often more than a third, were involved in the building, clothing, or food and drink trades. But there were also relatively specialist jobs like those of bookseller and stationer which appear in the major Kentish towns towards the middle of our period: Jacobean Canterbury had two or three stationers, as well as other traders who dabbled in the book-trade on the side. Innkeepers and victuallers were another rising group in the occupational hierarchy. Together with this specialist service-sector there was usually a group of industrial trades. Most of the larger country towns retained some kind of industrial function into the seventeenth century, typically a woollen textile industry as at Gloucester, Shrewsbury, and Salisbury—though this was often in decline. At Leicester there was a busy tanning industry located by the river just outside the north gate. In addition, of course, some of the greater county towns, like Southampton and Chester, doubled as ports, with a role in international and overseas trade.

The economy of the county town was thus more varied and diverse than that of the market centre. It was also more rigidly organized. Almost all county towns in the sixteenth century had a large array of craft gilds. Prior to the Reformation these had usually possessed a religious motif, but from the 1540s they were primarily concerned with economic (and to a lesser extent political) regulation. In a provincial city like Chester there were at least twenty-five gilds in the sixteenth century, and even in a smaller county town like Lincoln there were half as many. In conjunction with the magistracy the gilds controlled craft apprenticeships, standards of workmanship, and competition among the masters; they also prosecuted outsiders infringing their trade monopoly. In the later

Middle Ages the craft gilds had often functioned as secondary, relatively autonomous, centres of political power but by 1600 they were closely integrated with civic administration. In many communities they were little more than auxiliary weapons of the town oligarchy, as at Maidstone where the gild wardens were employed to patrol the town, suppress disorder, and eject undesirables.

Nevertheless, despite the waning significance of the gilds, the political organization of the county towns remained highly complex. The political function of urban communities in this period will be examined in some detail in chapter nine, but it is important to stress here the wide variety of civic organs in the county towns. Many had received royal grants of incorporation, and the Tudor period in particular saw a host of new charters, both extending borough status to rising market-towns and enlarging the rights and privileges of established municipalities. In consequence the great majority of county towns had a multiplicity of courts—biennial leets, courts of pleas, market courts, quarter sessions—as well as the central town council. The latter was normally bi-cameral, with the mayor and senior magistrates on one side and the common councillors on the other. In most boroughs the members of the corporation were co-opted from a larger group of freemen, who in turn were drawn from the much greater number of unenfranchised townsmen. Not only was the political structure of most boroughs complex and élitist, but there was a bewildering degree of institutional variation from one county town to the next. Civic peculiarities of this sort served as an emblem of town autonomy. No less important, they helped to buttress the position of the local political establishment: the more individual and particularist the institutions and route to power, the greater the advantage of those townsmen familiar with them. Compared to the market-town, politics in the established county centre was very much a closed shop.

Royal charters also gave county towns a considerable measure of formal autonomy in their relations with outsiders. They were often exempted from the control of county sessions and from the activities of the county sheriff. In some cases this independence from county jurisdiction was further enhanced by charters making the town a county in its own right: Gloucester acquired this status in 1605 and Worcester in 1621; by 1660 there were sixteen county boroughs in England. In the later Middle Ages borough charters, backed by the force of town walls, allowed many larger urban communities to stand aside from seigneurial faction-fighting, while their right to elect parliamentary burgesses gave them at least some voice at the centre. But after 1500 civic independence of this sort steadily declined. The Crown and county landowners made increasing inroads into town liberties and the right to elect M.P.s, already coveted by fifteenth-century gentry, was now largely usurped by Tudor landowners.

This brings us to the role of the county town as a centre of particular ideas and values. At the close of the Middle Ages, the county town, encircled by its impressive line of walls, regarded itself and was regarded by outsiders as a cultural commonwealth, *sui generis*, quite separate from the common run of market-towns and villages, distinct even from other cities in the same urban class. Citizens of the larger towns were united by the more or less elaborate fabric of civic ceremony, invariably with a substantial religious content. The pervasive religious atmosphere was sustained by a variety of ecclesiastical institutions, monastic houses, parish churches, and chantries, whose buildings dominated the urban horizon. With the Reformation, however, this quali-tative difference between the cultural roles of the county and market-towns began to fade. Those striking cultural features of the pre-1640 town—the Puritan lectureship and the town grammar school—were common both to the borough and to the market centre. Numerous larger towns even lost the physical distinction of their town walls, which now fell into decay. The main difference between the two types of town was more quantitative than qualitative in this period. County towns could usually support not one, but a chorus of Puritan preachers, while their grammar schools were ordinarily supplied by numerous elementary schools. Thus, at Canterbury in the early seventeenth century, the endowed secondary school was able to recruit from between twenty and thirty petty schools in the city. Not surprisingly, the general influence of the county town on the adjoining countryside tended to be more extensive than that of the market-town.

As the preceding analysis will have suggested, the period from 1500 to 1700 was in many ways a time of difficulty for most old-established cities and medium-sized towns. The early decades of the sixteenth century heard a litany of protest and complaint about declining industries and trade, while the 1540 act for the 're-edifying' of decayed towns listed such places as Canterbury, Coventry, Chichester, Salisbury, Winchester, Hereford, Colchester, Rochester, Worcester, Stafford, Southampton, and Oxford. The Elizabethan period may have seen some limited revival in their fortunes. Their populations began to expand; their merchants began to exploit the growing agrarian prosperity and the development of domestic trade; their cultural influence may have revived. But all the signs are that the overall stabilization, if not improvement in their position, did not continue into the seventeenth century. Stafford, for example, despite a mild recovery during Elizabeth's reign, was by the middle of the seventeenth century clearly suffering from general stagnation affecting most aspects of urban life. Stagnation was not universal: most counties had one larger town which now became *the* county centre, monopolizing its trade and serving as the focus of its social life. In the 1670s Thomas Baskerville described Nottingham, for example, as 'Paradise restored, for here you find large streets, fair-built houses, fine women, and many coaches rattling about, and their shops full of merchantable goods.' But this limited success was usually gained at the expense of other middling and smaller centres. And, as we shall see, even the successful county town was by 1700 only a shadow of the late medieval civic commonwealth: its political, cultural, and even to some extent its economic importance was not of its own making.

When we investigate the reasons for the vicissitudes of the county town, it is clear that at least some of them had also affected the fortunes of the market-town. However, the impact was often quite different. Whereas the general population increase of the sixteenth century had improved the position of the market-town, it frequently caused critical problems for the older middling centres. It is true that the latter benefited from the demand-led expansion of internal trade, mainly in the late sixteenth century, but this gain was more than offset by the great influx of rural poor, tramping in from the countryside and threatening the economic, social, and political fabric of the community. Again, while the growth of political peace and stability aided the market-towns, it exposed the larger centres to the intervention of a centralizing Crown and its agents, the county gentry.

At the same time, the older county centres were affected by changes which had only a limited impact on the market-town. The most significant, as we shall see in chapter ten, was the Reformation. Given the importance of religious institutions to the late medieval community, it was inevitable that their destruction or remodelling in the 1530s and 1540s should have inflicted permanent damage on the traditional, particularist sense of civic identity. Since religious houses were often a major source of urban revenue, their dissolution also seriously undermined the economy of numerous middling towns. Abingdon, for instance, complained bitterly after the dissolution of its abbey that 'the town is sore decayed and like daily more to decay'.

In the short run, the small and medium-sized provincial towns had markedly different careers for much of our period. While the former had tended to prosper before 1640, many of the latter had been able to earn no more than temporary remission in their general decline. But by 1700 both classes of town were in the same boat, their prospects equally gloomy, faced as they were by a powerful set of urban competitors, including the new towns.

3

New Towns

One of the striking features of English urban society in our period was the development of a variety of communities with new functions and structures: spas, dockyard towns, and industrial centres. By 1700 there were nearly thirty new towns. The precise pattern of development varied a good deal according to the town's specialist function. But it is possible to construct a general model of the urban characteristics of these new centres which is in sharp contrast to the profile of the traditional towns which we examined in the preceding chapter.

Let us start with the spa towns. There had, of course, been English medicinal wells and springs since the Roman period, but the spa town with its combination of curative and leisure activities did not really make its appearance until after 1600. The idea, like the word, may have been imported from the Low Countries and Germany, to which a considerable number of English gentry journeyed to take the waters in the late sixteenth and early seventeenth centuries. With the Thirty Years War foreign travel was curtailed, creating the need for English surrogates. Within two generations there were as many as a dozen spa towns of varying significance. Among the most important were Bath, Epsom Wells, Tunbridge Wells, Buxton, and Scarborough. Bath's population may have already been about 3,000 in 1700, but most spa centres had fewer inhabitants. During the season, however, spa populations probably doubled as the well-to-do, their servants, and a host of dependent traders, physicians, and the like flocked to the waters.

Needless to say, the basic prerequisite of the spa was a

spring with supposed medicinal qualities. At Bath, the baths were of Roman origin. With the dissolution of Bath Abbey, the five main ones had passed under civic control, and by the 1620s they were attracting a small but steady stream of gentle customers. In 1628 Thomas Venner noted the practice of frequenting the baths in spring and autumn, adding that the city was 'beautified with fair and goodly buildings for receipt of strangers'. Nonetheless, bathing may still have been a somewhat hazardous exercise, since in 1646 it was said that 'dogs, cats, pigs and even human creatures were hurled over the rails into the water while people were bathing in it'. No wonder that a growing number of visitors preferred simply to drink the spring water. A mixture of drinking and bathing seems also to have occurred at other spa centres like Buxton and Scarborough. In the latter, bathing was mostly confined to the springs until the mid-eighteenth century when the new fashion for sea-bathing took over. Imbibing the waters was not always more pleasant than immersion, however: even Celia Fiennes, an incorrigible spa visitor, complained of the noxious taste of the drink at Buxton.

As well as a medicinal spring the spa town needed publicity. Medical backing was especially valuable. Dr. William Turner's pamphlet on the therapeutic powers of the Bath waters, published in 1562, provided an important early boost to the town's growth as a spa centre, while Dr. Ludowick Rowzee's treatise on the Tunbridge waters during the 1630s quickly put the Kent spa on the social map. In 1705 there was a pamphlet war between physicians from Bath and Tunbridge Wells in which the protagonists loudly praised the curative excellence of their home spas and derided their rival's claims. By the end of the seventeenth century most of the larger centres had groups of medical practitioners servicing the visitors. In this respect the spas were an important beneficiary, if not a manifestation, of the growing importance of the medical profession in the seventeenth century.

At the same time, if a spa was really to succeed it needed upper class patronage. A royal visit might well make a spa's reputation for good. Bath was especially favoured, with visits by Charles II's queen in 1663, James II's queen in 1687 and

Queen Anne in 1702–3; Tunbridge Wells had to be content
with repeated royal visits during the 1660s. With these seals of
Crown approval both towns were able to attract the cream of
spa visitors, including the aristocracy. Other spas prospered
with a less grand clientele. In 1705 James Taylor wrote of
Scarborough: 'the most of the gentry of the North of England
and Scotland resort hither in the season of the year.' Gentry
mobility was encouraged by increased landed prosperity and
by transport improvements like the coach, the road book,
and (from the 1690s) the turnpike. Travel to the more liberal
atmosphere of the spa may also have reflected the gentry's
desire to overturn those Puritan constraints on social behaviour which had been discredited by the English Revolution.
John Macky noted that one of the attractions of Epsom Wells
was Box Hill, where it was easy for 'gentlemen and ladies
insensibly to lose their company in these pretty labyrinths of
box-wood and divert themselves unperceived', so that 'it may
justly be called the Palace of Venus'.

Leisure facilities varied to some extent according to the
clientele. At aristocratic Bath there were assembly rooms for
dancing, gaming, and music, though as yet there was little of
the ritualized etiquette and entertainment that one associates
with Beau Nash and the Georgian spa. Epsom Wells was
rather less select and its facilities less sophisticated. Celia
Fiennes noted 'a coffee house and two rooms for gaming and
shops for sweetmeats and fruit'. The company paraded
around the two greens in the town and also went racing on
Banstead down. At Scarborough, conditions were much more
primitive and provincial, with daily walks along the sea shore
one of the few recognized diversions, although by 1700 the
town could at least boast the luxury of a purpose-built spa-
house run by a self-styled northern 'wit'.

Most spa entertainments were modelled on those fashionable in London society. At the coffee house, for instance,
gentlemen might read the latest London news or hear the
latest London gossip. Significantly a number of spa centres,
particularly Epsom and Tunbridge Wells, were reasonably
close to the capital. According to Celia Fiennes visitors to
Epsom frequently came up for a long weekend, staying from

Saturday through to Tuesday and then returning to London for the rest of the week. Commuting like this was no doubt exceptional, but it underlines the essential point that the later Stuart spas were primarily offshoots of the metropolis, drawing their inspiration from London high society. They were holiday camps for the landed élite and commercial tycoons who now dominated the capital. As such they provided light relief, with their sense of camping out, from the fashionable rigours of the London season. For those northern landowners unable to get down to the metropolis, the jollifications at Scarborough were the next best thing.

It would be wrong to stress the novel character of the spa town to the exclusion of its more traditional aspects. Several of the spas had important markets; Bath and Scarborough retained a residual array of ordinary trades (Bath had once been an active textile centre); one or two were still ruled by an orthodox civic magistracy. But in most cases these traditional features were increasingly overshadowed by the town's new leisure industry. At Tunbridge Wells, for example, the market, 'furnished with great plenty of all sorts, flesh, fowl and fish', was geared almost exclusively to the provisioning of spa visitors. In the main, the spas were urban communities of a new style, with characteristics distinct from those of the more traditional town.

The dockyard towns, like the spas, were mainly a product of the Stuart period. During the sixteenth century the main royal dockyards had been at Deptford and Woolwich on the Thames, and these continued to expand steadily thereafter. But from the 1620s they were also joined by a number of other provincial centres with better, more accessible yards. By 1640 Chatham, at the mouth of the river Medway, was firmly established as the leading government dockyard, complete with a complex range of dry-docks, forts, and other works. Portsmouth was another new centre: here the main expansion occurred during the Cromwellian wars of the 1650s and the Anglo-French struggles of the 1690s. Other, lesser dockyard towns of the later seventeenth century included Falmouth, Plymouth Dock, Sheerness (mainly an

advance base for Chatham), and Harwich. The populations
of the dockyard towns are difficult to estimate, not least
because of their sharp fluctuations, both annual and seasonal,
in response to the changing pressure of military activity.
Deptford probably had a fairly constant population of
4–5,000 by the 1660s, while Chatham may have increased
the number of its inhabitants from under 1,000 in 1600 to
over 5,000 a century later.

Military factors were obviously vital in the location and
development of the dockyard towns. Chatham, for instance,
not only provided more accessible yards for large warships
than its up-river competitors, but its position at the junction
of the Medway and the Thames estuaries made it an in-
valuable base for the defence of the Home Counties and
London—a point confirmed by the Dutch attack in 1667.
Portsmouth similarly functioned both as an important centre
for the Channel fleet, guarding the western approaches, and
as a stronghold against foreign attack on the south coast,
protecting the vulnerable area of the Solent.

Military factors were not the only determinants of these
new urban developments, however. In most cases the towns
were able to exploit hinterlands with abundant supplies of
naval materials. From the close of the sixteenth century we
have evidence of dockyard officials moving up the Medway
estuary purchasing cordage, timber, and ordnance, the latter
from the Wealden iron industry. By 1700 the dockyard town
controlled an extensive network of contractors and suppliers
throughout much of mid-Kent. The same hinterland with its
declining textile manufactures and stagnant agriculture (at
least after 1660) also served as an important recruiting area
for the dockyard labour force. The influx of workers probably reached its peak with the wars after 1688: in 1704 there
were over 3,000 men employed by the government in the
Kent yards alone.

By 1700 therefore the dockyard towns were centres of
rapid growth based on a single industry, having much in
common, as we shall see, with the new industrial communities of the North and the Midlands. This is not to
say that they lacked all the characteristics of the traditional

town. At Portsmouth, for instance, while the royal dock-yards increasingly overshadowed the urban economy and led to housing development outside the old city limits, the town was still administered by a conventional corporate magistracy. At Chatham the townsmen had some access to the markets, schools, and other services of the ancient city of Rochester next door. As with the spa towns, how-ever, these were residual features of declining significance compared with the novel dominance of a single specialized activity.

Our third group of new towns—the industrial centres—was the largest. By 1700 there were at least a dozen new industrial centres, ranging from major settlements like Birmingham and Leeds with 7–8,000 inhabitants down to lesser communities such as Sheffield with fewer than 3,500. Some of these towns could trace their industrial pedigree back to the sixteenth century or earlier. Thus John Leland wrote of Birmingham in the 1530s that 'a great part of the town is maintained by smiths who have their iron and sea-coal out of Staffordshire'. But in almost all these centres specialized industrial growth was a phenomenon of the Stuart rather than the Tudor period. *Pace* Leland, Birmingham's inhabi-tants were engaged in tanning and agriculture, as well as metal-work, before 1600. It was only thereafter that the leading families increasingly concentrated on metal manu-facture and trading, taking advantage of the migration into the vicinity of iron foundries which had been forced out of Cannock Chase by the exhaustion of fuel supplies there. Within a generation, the town was not only a major industrial centre but also the leading trade outlet for metal products made in the villages of the Midland Plain. By 1650 the same industrial specialization was also evident at Manchester, whose trade was then described as 'not inferior to that of many cities in the kingdom, chiefly consisting in woollen friezes, fustians, sack-cloths, mingled stuffs, caps, inkles, tapes, points etc., whereby not only the better sort of men are employed but also the very children by their own labour can maintain themselves.' At the start of the eighteenth century the geographical distribution of English industrial towns was firmly established with the highest density of centres in the North and the Midlands.

How do we explain the growth and location of these new industrial towns? Proximity to raw materials was clearly important in many cases. The Midland communities of Birmingham, Walsall, and Wednesbury, for example, were able to make use of local supplies of iron-ore, coal, and timber for their metal manufacture, while the Yorkshire woollen towns, turning out cheap rough cloths, largely depended on the coarse wool grown on the wolds and moors. The Yorkshire clothiers also utilized the water power of upland streams to drive the fulling mills which beat and cleansed their cloth. Water was equally important as a form of transport and good river communication was of vital significance in opening up the West Midlands as an industrial area: by the later 1630s the Avon was made navigable as far as Stratford on Avon and the late seventeenth century saw further attempts to improve the other tributaries of the Severn.

In addition there were a number of specifically urban factors involved in the growth of the new centres. One was the absence of the high civic overheads which were an inevitable consequence of the elaborate paraphernalia of the corporate town which we described in chapter two. The citizens of Norwich, for example, complained in 1531 that membership of the city gilds was so burdensome that 'many of them that did bear the charges of such gilds could not after that recover [their] great losses . . . by occasion whereof many of them fled and daily went from the said city.' It was not merely the high costs of corporate life which the trader avoided in the new urban centre. There were none of the controls on competition and labour supply which raised wages and reduced productivity in the older centres. According to some accounts, food prices were lower outside the regulated markets of the cities, thereby giving manu-facturers in the new industrial towns a further competitive edge so far as labour costs were concerned. Certainly workers in the smaller industrial towns often retained an interest in agriculture, to which they returned during periods of slack trade. The openness and flexibility of the new industrial centres was celebrated by the Victorian Liberal, J. T. Bunce, who declared that 'the great glory of Birmingham, the source of its strength and the cause of its rapid advance in prosperity and population was that it was a free town. Neither personal nor corporate hindrances existed in it.' Significantly, the older corporate towns resisted the development of industry in the neighbouring countryside, whereas the new industrial towns appear to have encouraged and promoted village production. In this way town traders found extra sources of supply and also, in return, a growing market for their retail trade.

As with the spas and dockyard centres, it would be wrong to focus entirely on the novel features of the industrial towns. Some of them, like Birmingham and Wolverhampton, had grown out of long-established market-towns and owed much of their new importance to the entrepreneurial opportunities which marketing networks had provided. A number had at least some of the trappings of the older country towns: Leeds, for instance, was chartered in 1626 with an oligarchic mayor and aldermen, and there were various attempts to establish a strictly regulated textile industry there. But by 1700 most of these more orthodox urban characteristics were fading into insignificance. At Leeds the Caroline corporation aroused fierce opposition from lesser clothiers and during the 1640s lapsed for a time. Though subsequently revived, it appears not to have exercised any rigorous control over the economic life of the town. Interestingly enough, even older provincial centres like Norwich, which retained a major industrial function in 1700, experienced some liberalization of their traditional structure, the ruling élite becoming more open, embracing new men and new trades. In spite of exceptions like Norwich and Colchester, however, there can be little question that by the early eighteenth century most industrial activity was swinging away from the medieval network of urban communities in the south and east towards the new centres further north.

So far, we have been mainly concerned with exploring the diversity of factors affecting the growth of the various types of new town in the Stuart period. We have also suggested that, although they often retained lineaments of the more traditional kind of urban community, these were usually of little significance by 1700. We must now look more closely at some of the basic features which were common to all the new urban centres and which, taken together, indicate the development of a form of urban society quite different from that of the traditional country towns.

The most striking aspect of the new towns was the predominance of a single type of economic activity, whether entertaining spa visitors, building warships, or making brassware or cheap cloths. There was little of the mixed economy of marketing, services, and crafts which was prevalent in other provincial towns by 1700. Related to the heavy economic specialization of the industrial and dockyard towns was their growing reliance on large units of production: at Chatham alone, the dry-docks and other facilities were worth over £56,000 by 1698. As a result these towns tended to be highly vulnerable to short-term economic fluctuations. The fortunes of the dockyard towns rose or fell quite dramatically according to the dictates of war or peace: peace was usually punctuated by cries of anguish from unemployed shipwrights. Trade fluctuations had an equally disruptive impact on the industrial towns, especially textile centres like Halifax, where it was said that the parish was 'so barren and unfruitful as it will not suffice to yield victuals for the third part of the inhabitants, and the poor that spin the wool there . . . cannot gain for their labour four pence a day towards their living.'

The specialist economic function of the new towns was not their only distinctive feature. By comparison with the typical country town they usually had a dispersed population and topography. At Tunbridge Wells, for example, the logical area for building was in the vicinity of the well, but the new houses which sprang up from the 1680s tended to sprawl along the Southborough road and on the north side of the town common. Part of the explanation was the refusal of the manorial freeholders, who controlled the common near the well, to lease out the land for development. But it also reflected the absence of an effective municipal administration, capable of overruling private interests in the cause of public need and concerned to see the town develop as an integrated, coherent community. The landscape of the Stuart dockyard town was also disorderly, its housing having developed higgledy-piggledy in periods of economic boom. John Philipott commented in 1659 that Deptford was dominated by a recent mass of 'small tenements', while a modern study of Chatham has suggested that it was 'a shapeless agglomeration of dwellings, most of them shabby'. Many of the industrial centres had grown in all directions out of small market-towns, large villages, or even groups of settlements, presenting a picture of uncontrolled industrial blight. Defoe described Sheffield as 'very populous and large, the streets narrow and the houses dark and black, occasioned by the continued smoke of the forges.'

Not all new towns experienced this unplanned growth. The colliery centre of Whitehaven on the Cumberland coast, which developed rapidly from the 1680s, followed a gridiron pattern of streets with the quality of the housing carefully supervised. But this was the result, not of communal initiative, but of the grand design of the colliery owner and paternalist landlord, Sir John Lowther, who declared his aim of 'building a regular town'. At Portsea the new tenements erected after 1700 also achieved a certain, largely accidental, regularity as a consequence of building on the original open-field strips, not from any coherent plan.

With their growing populations the new towns all relied heavily on immigration from the countryside. In the case of the spas this was mostly respectable, upper-class migration, although there was a growing influx of the parasitical poor— beggars, tricksters, and the like, hoping to cadge from the rich on holiday. But the vast majority of immigrants into the dockyard and industrial towns were the labouring poor, attracted relatively long distances by the towns' reputations as places of employment and prosperity. A substantial number of the workmen at Chatham probably came from London, while migrants to Birmingham in the late seventeenth century included not only a large number from the neighbouring counties of Warwickshire, Worcestershire, and Staffordshire, but also a significant group (by 1700 nearly a quarter) from further afield, from Gloucestershire, Oxford-shire, and Leicestershire. Although our evidence is less complete, Manchester probably recruited many of its late seventeenth-century inhabitants from the uplands of Lanca-shire, Yorkshire, and Cumberland; a number doubtless came from the smaller market centres whose later Stuart decline we noted in chapter two. The high incidence of mobility into the new towns was in sharp contrast to the general picture presented by other provincial towns in the late seventeenth century. There the number of immigrants was declining and most movement was over short distances. To some extent this reflected the diminished economic attraction of the older provincial centres, but it was also the result of stricter and more rigorously enforced settlement regulations in the older towns compared with the new centres.

This absence of effective municipal controls was another striking feature of most new towns. Not surprisingly, it seriously reduced their ability to cope with the social problems created by rapid economic and demographic growth. From the 1590s the Manchester court leet, the town's only administrative body, was presented with constant com-plaints about the number of poor immigrants, all to no avail. In 1670 there were reports of 'the frequent coming in of journeymen, foreigners, strangers, sojourners, wandering and idle persons from remote and adjacent parts', who were lodged in alehouses and tenements. By 1700 most of the dockyard and industrial towns had large numbers of paupers living in acute squalor, sleeping in cellars or on the streets. Poor relief was rudimentary and unable to cope with the wild fluctua-tions of economic activity. Chatham's frequent pleas for help in relieving its poor had to be referred to the tardy debate of county justices meeting miles away at Maidstone. Sanitation was often non-existent and disorder endemic. In 1687 Brad-ford manorial court denounced the 'young women healthful and strong' who 'combine and agree to cot and live together without government and . . . give great occasion for lewdness.'

Failure to impose effective social control was an inevitable result of the lack of a sophisticated administrative and political apparatus in most new towns. In the majority of cases the administrative mechanism was hardly more advanced than that of a small market-town. Manchester, for example, with a population of nearly 9,000 in 1700, was loosely controlled by the court leet meeting at Easter and Michaelmas under a high bailiff and a low bailiff. It is true that by the 1670s the leet nominally appointed as many as one hundred officials, from constables and market wardens to 'officers for muzzling mastiff dogs'. But given the infrequent meetings of the court it is hardly surprising that local officials never got to grips with the mounting problems of the new town. At Bradford and Birmingham there were similar, if more primitive, manorial regimes, while at Sheffield urban authority, such as it was, was vested after 1681 in a committee of feoffees. Elsewhere town business was probably run by local oligarchies operating as parish vestries. The simple administrative mechanism of most new towns, their lack of civic autonomy and parliamentary representation, were all in striking contrast to the complex political and administrative structures of the older established centres.

The new towns were rather closer to the old in their wider role as centres of religion, education, and other cultural activities. Birmingham, Manchester, Leeds, Deptford, and possibly Chatham were active centres of religious radicalism in the seventeenth century. Manchester was the lynch-pin of the Presbyterian classis or church organization in mid-seventeenth century Lancashire; Birmingham was a leading separatist centre both before and during the Civil War; while the Kentish dockyard towns contained various sects from whom John Lilburne may have recruited Leveller support in the 1640s. Manchester, Birmingham, Leeds, and Bradford had important grammar schools, and in the late seventeenth century the spas were famous as centres of high fashion and the latest taste. Soon after 1700 Claver Morris, a surgeon from Wells, hurried off to Bath to listen to the most fashionable Italian composers and bring back their music for his local choral society.

Yet it would be wrong to think of the new towns as exerting a major or distinctive cultural role in the wider community. It is true that their religious radicalism often had strong local roots, encouraged by the inadequacy of orthodox, ecclesiastical institutions. Many industrial centres had to make do with a chapelry, or at best a single parish church, well into the eighteenth century. Even Tunbridge Wells had no church at all until the 1680s, when a small brick structure was erected by wealthy spa visitors. But religious dissent may sometimes have been a reflection less of urban opinion than of the forceful attitudes of local landowners. In post-Reformation Manchester, the Dissenting interest relied heavily on the powerful Wharton family, great county magnates, while many of the townsfolk themselves, often recent migrants from the Catholic countryside, were conservative to the point of Jacobitism. As for the grammar schools founded in the larger towns, they, too, often depended on outside support: thus at Manchester the school's feoffees after 1660 were mostly county gentry. The wider cultural impact of the new towns had to wait until the eighteenth century. The Italian music which Claver Morris enjoyed at Bath had come down second-hand from the salons of the metropolis.

The new towns of seventeenth-century England had a positive and relatively distinct urban profile. Many of their economic, political, and social features clearly differentiated them from the main run of established provincial towns. The foundations for their later development, which would transform the face of English urban society in the eighteenth century, can already be discerned in 1700. But we should beware of antedating their importance. Birmingham, the largest of the new towns, still had only one-third of the population of the old provincial city of Norwich. In spite of their recent growth the majority of the new towns had populations of less than 5,000, and overall they housed little more than 12 per cent of the total English population living in towns. At the end of our period the main impetus of urban development was to be found elsewhere, in the major established cities—the provincial capitals, the great ports, and London.

4

Provincial Capitals

As we noted earlier, there was a small group of English towns whose size, sophistication, and influence beyond their own boundaries set them apart from other urban communities. These were the provincial capitals, the foci of regions larger than single counties, which—though they were of distinctly smaller size and significance than London—nevertheless deserve separate consideration as representatives of English urban society in its most developed form.

Five towns, without question, held this position throughout our period. Bristol and York had been centres of life in the west and the north since the early Middle Ages, the only 'towns of importance in the kingdom' apart from London, according to one Italian visitor in 1500. But already in the same league were Norwich, the undisputed capital of East Anglia in the later Middle Ages, and Exeter and Newcastle, which had carved out for themselves positions of significance and wealth in the far west and far north before 1500; Newcastle was already the third richest provincial town (after Bristol and York) in 1334. These five towns with populations of between 8,000 and 12,000 in the 1520s were still the most populous provincial towns in the 1660s, the number of inhabitants ranging from about 20,000 in Norwich to 12,000 in York. Compared with some of the major provincial towns of continental Europe (both Rouen and Toulouse had populations of over 40,000 in the early sixteenth century) they were not large. But they exercised an unquestioned dominance in provincial England and the fact of their continuing leadership over two centuries is itself a sign of their resilience and reserves of power, allowing them to ride out the economic and social pressures which adversely affected so many smaller towns.

Other towns came near to occupying a position of similar eminence in the course of our period. In 1500 Salisbury and Coventry were large and wealthy enough, but in both cases the sixteenth century saw their industries decay and their populations fall. Significantly, neither the Midlands nor the southern counties produced a single provincial capital, partly because they were too close to London to escape the effects of its growth as a port and distributive centre, and partly because there were too many towns ready to compete for the position—Salisbury, Reading and Southampton, Coventry, Leicester, Northampton, and later Birmingham. In the Welsh Marches, too, neither Worcester, Gloucester, nor Shrewsbury was big enough to dominate the others and none of them had the paramount advantage of being a significant port. It is striking that several of the towns which rose towards the top of the provincial hierarchy in the seventeenth century were major ports and that, like the existing provincial capitals, they were well away from London. Liverpool we know was expanding rapidly in the later seventeenth century, though its population in 1700 was as yet only a little over 5,000 and Chester was still its urban rival. But the growth of Hull (8,000) and Plymouth (over 9,000) had pushed them further up the scale. Already there were signs of the rapid urban developments of the eighteenth century. But in 1700 the front rank was still occupied by Norwich, Bristol, Exeter, York, and Newcastle. They held a stable position in an otherwise changing urban hierarchy, and it is their persistence as the major English provincial towns that we must seek to explain in this chapter.

Some of the variables determining the location and success of these centres have already been listed in the context of the country towns. The advantages they conferred were different in scale, not in kind. The provincial capitals were all at nodal points of transport networks, especially those formed by navigable rivers, which gave them access to large hinterlands. Bristol and York benefited most in this respect. The Ouse and its tributaries, leading into the North and West Ridings, to

Hull and the sea, and via the Trent to the Midlands, made York a natural point for the exchange of goods from different local economies. The Severn and its estuary, the Wye and the Avon, gave Bristol equal opportunities. The Severn was the only great English river whose navigation was not impeded by weirs, floodgates, and locks, and it was said in 1635 to be navigable as far as Shrewsbury. Exeter and Norwich depended less on rivers for contact with the populous and increasingly industrial areas which surrounded them, but they relied heavily on water-carriage with their ports at Topsham and Yarmouth, while the importance for Newcastle of the Tyne needs no stressing. The upkeep and improvement of waterways therefore played a major part in the life of these towns. There were frequent projects for canals, constant disputes with local landowners whose weirs impeded navigation, and vigorous interference in the activities of local authorities appointed to conserve rivers like the Tyne and the Ouse.

Marketing and inland trade were as basic to the existence of provincial capitals as to that of smaller towns. But the market areas were much larger and the goods exchanged more diverse. Consequently these centres were less vulnerable to the vicissitudes of purely local consumer demand than their lesser neighbours. York, for example, provided corn for the West Riding towns from the fertile arable lands of Holderness, Lincolnshire, and East Anglia, just as Newcastle served as a distribution point for grain (imported from King's Lynn) over much of the pastoral North. York's pewterers and goldsmiths catered for a wide market throughout the northern counties while the city also functioned as a provincial entrepôt for specialized consumer goods from London. Its markets for malt, leather, fish, cattle, pigs, and West Riding and Kendal cloth gave it a permanent commercial predominance over lesser market-towns like Tadcaster and Selby. In the same fashion Norwich specialized as a marketing centre for grain and livestock: the latter were fattened in the marshes to the east of the city, then sold to London dealers. Norwich merchants also distributed heavy goods and groceries throughout Norfolk. Bristol had similar functions, reaching a wide area through its imports of industrial raw materials, especially iron and woad. The economic pull of these centres was most strikingly demonstrated at the great fairs they sponsored, like the three-day Lammas fair at York and the St. James's and St. Paul's fairs in Bristol, which drew customers from all over the West Country and South Wales.

In addition, these towns were all important political and ecclesiastical centres. In 1500 Newcastle still retained its vital role as a fortress against the Scots, while the castles and walls of the others displayed their original strategic importance—to be demonstrated again during the campaigns of the Civil War. All of them, except Newcastle (and Bristol before 1540), were the seats of bishops, and all had acquired rich monasteries, numerous chantries, and impressive parish churches in the Middle Ages. Most of the regional capitals also enjoyed political prestige as county towns, the meeting places of quarter sessions and assizes, centres for the mustering of the local militias, and the collection of taxes. York in particular was a real capital city for the North for most of our period, the seat of the Council in the North, established at the King's Manor in 1561, and of the Ecclesiastical Commission for the Northern Province. The judicial business of its courts brought litigants in their hundreds from all over the northern counties.

Large though they were, the provincial capitals also resembled smaller towns in not being totally divorced from rural life. A countryman might cross them on foot in a few minutes. There were only ninety-three acres within the walls of Exeter, although it had growing suburbs outside its gates, and Norwich, one of the biggest walled towns, covered less than a square mile. Their precincts contained extensive open spaces, fields and meadows, like the Gildencroft in Norwich or those in the Redcliffe quarter of Bristol, and gardens such as those attached to Bedford House in the south-east corner of Exeter. The existence of *rus in urbe* was also demonstrated in the activities of the citizens, who turned out for harvest work, kept pigs and poultry, and if they were rich enough, owned rural property. Some of the wealthiest men in Tudor

Newcastle, for example, were butchers who also acted as graziers.

The provincial capitals thus shared many of the features of country towns. But there were three determinants of their position which set them qualitatively as well as quantitatively apart from smaller centres: their role in long-distance and overseas trade, their connections with specialist local industries, and their activity as social centres whose sophistication was excelled only by London. Not all of them fulfilled each of these functions at the same time. But the variety of economic activities potentially open to them contributed heavily to their prominence throughout our period, providing new sources of wealth when older ones declined.

It was long-distance trade which gave most of these provincial capitals their wide regional influence, dictating the rhythm and pattern of local economies through their export of local products and their import of raw materials and consumer goods. Although Norwich and York were not themselves ports, their merchants nevertheless engaged in trade through Yarmouth and Hull. The relationship between the two East Anglian towns has still to be fully explored, but throughout the sixteenth century York men dominated the trade and shipping of Hull, exporting lead and cloth and importing a more varied range of goods, including corn, flax, iron, wine, and oil. The York Merchant Adventurers, supported by their monopoly in the sale of imports (established by charter in 1581), were some of the richest men in the town. While Newcastle's trade involved other commodities such as salt and glass, it revolved around coal, catering for growing demand in London and in northern Europe. Shipments of coal from the town increased from about 35,000 tons per annum in the 1560s to over 500,000 tons in 1660, when local production exceeded that of all other European coalfields put together. This enormous volume of trade was closely controlled by the hostmen, recognized and constituted as a company by the town's charter of 1600. The trade of Exeter, 'the emporium of the western parts', lay in the sixteenth century largely with France, West Country cloth being exchanged for canvas, linen, wine, and a host of commodities from starch to playing cards; again the profits were in the hands of a company of Merchant Adventurers, chartered and granted a monopoly of the French trade in 1559. Bristol too had its own company of Merchant Venturers, chartered in 1552, with exclusive control of an even more diverse trade with southern Europe, supplying raw materials and consumer goods for much of the West Country and Wales. This company gradually engrossed the trade of lesser ports on the Bristol Channel like Minehead, Barnstaple, and Bideford.

The commerce of the provincial capitals was not always prosperous, however. It suffered from the general commercial crises of the mid-sixteenth century (caused by foreign wars and changing conditions in overseas markets) and it underwent important, structural adjustments in the seventeenth century. For much of the period severe economic fluctuations meant that merchant fortunes, though often large, were not secure. Wars abroad in the 1620s and at home in the 1640s seriously disrupted the trade of Bristol and Exeter. In the latter, the volume of commerce may have fallen by as much as two-thirds in the course of the 1620s. But the 'Commercial Revolution' of the later seventeenth century gave the major ports new openings and fresh prosperity. The benefits were not confined to the older centres of trade. Just as Liverpool expanded as an outlet for Lancashire textiles and a source of Irish and colonial imports, so Hull rose as an exporter of West Riding cloth and a centre of trade with the Baltic after the Navigation Acts of 1651 and 1660 had excluded Dutch competition. Its new greatness was independent of York, which alone among the old provincial capitals failed to profit from the expansion of overseas trade after the Restoration.

By contrast, Exeter and Bristol did particularly well. Commerce between Exeter and southern Europe had declined before the Civil War, but the city's trade was revitalized after 1660 by the growth in exports of serges to the Netherlands and in imports of linen and luxury goods, by its increasing mastery of the coastal trade from Plymouth to London, and by the activity of some Exeter men in the Newfoundland fisheries. This commercial diversification was accompanied by a significant shift in mercantile attitudes away from concern with monopoly control of a single commercial sector towards free trade: the Exeter Merchant Adventurers declined as an exclusive commercial caucus while parliamentary statutes of 1688 and 1697 opened up other branches of overseas trade hitherto dominated by London. Bristol profited from the addition of transatlantic commerce, especially in sugar and tobacco, to its older trades with Ireland and southern Europe. The volume of shipping entering the port from the West Indies rose from 1,900 tons in 1670 to 5,200 tons in 1700, and the number of ships from Virginia doubled between 1660 and the end of the century. Again this expansion may have been helped by the attitude of its merchants: the Merchant Venturers of Bristol were more outward looking and less exclusive than similar companies elsewhere. But it rested essentially on the town's large hinterland of consumers. According to Defoe, Bristol's ability to trade 'with a more entire independency upon London than any other town' stemmed from the fact that 'whatsoever exportations they make to any part of the world, they are able to bring the full returns back to their own port and can dispose of it there'.

The fortunes of the provincial capitals in overseas trade were closely dependent on their connections with specialized industries, and here, too, there were periods of crisis and significant changes of direction in the course of our period. All of them had been significant cloth-making centres during the later Middle Ages, but these industries were in decline in the early sixteenth century. Competition from Halifax, Leeds, and Wakefield, where wages and other costs were lower, had progressively eroded the fourteenth-century textile prosperity of York. There were complaints of decay from Bristol in the early sixteenth century and the export of Norwich worsteds slumped from 3,000 cloths at the beginning of the century to as few as thirty-eight in 1561. Only in York, however, were these setbacks decisive. There the weaving of worsted coverlets struggled on, aided by protectionist legislation in 1543; but, as we shall see, York had to look elsewhere for its economic recovery. The other provincial capitals were more successful in retaining their industrial interests or gaining new ones. Exeter adjusted to the growth of the cloth industry elsewhere in Devon by becoming the main county centre for the finishing rather than the manufacture of textiles: fulling and dyeing were increasingly important and profitable activities in the town. Bristol similarly engaged in the dyeing and dressing of cloths from the Wiltshire–Somerset border, and other industries dependent on the city's commerce, like soap manufacture and sugar-refining, flourished in the seventeenth century. In Newcastle the merchants and hostmen came to control the local coal industry, through their purchase of the Grand Lease of the mines in Gateshead and Whickham in 1583 and through the enterprise of individual families later.

The industrial importance of Norwich was most striking of all, for despite recurrent crises it remained a leading cloth-making centre. Its industry was revived in the first instance by the new draperies introduced by Dutch and Walloon refugees, and flourished between 1580 and 1620. But it expanded on an even greater scale after 1660 in response to rising domestic demand for specialized cloths, the famous Norwich 'stuffs'. The reasons for the continuing urban location of the textile industry in Norwich, in contrast to the experience of so many other towns which failed to resist rural competition, are still unclear. One factor may have been the importance in the city of a quite distinct immigrant community; another, perhaps, the relative openness of the city's trade structure in the later seventeenth century; a third may have been the city's skill in tapping particular sectors of domestic demand, helped by its own position as a leading commercial and distributive centre. But whatever the reasons, Norwich, unlike York, remained a major industrial town at the end of our period as it had been at the beginning.

Yet York was still a provincial capital and Norwich had continued to be one when its industry dwindled between 1520 and 1570. This was due to the third decisive element in the economic strength of all these towns: their role as social centres for their regions. Even in the early sixteenth century York had all the specialized trades and services which many county towns only began to acquire in the seventeenth. In 1510 a single York stationer was importing no less than 1,221 service books, for example, while the town's doctors, goldsmiths, horse-races and cockpits catered for the increasing numbers of country gentlemen drawn to the city by the growing business of its secular and ecclesiastical courts. Other occupations flourished in consequence: in 1577, for instance, the town contained a third of all the inns in Yorkshire. Even after the destruction of the Council in the North in 1641, York was still the leading social centre of northern England: at least 70 per cent of its workers were involved in servicing consumer demand, with much of this coming from visitors. Similar developments occurred in Norwich. The Duke of Norfolk held court there until 1570 and by then the town was becoming 'increasingly a centre of conspicuous consumption—a lesser London'. It was certainly this in the later Stuart period, with its 'Gentlemen's Walk' in the market-place, its grandiose mayoral inauguration aping the London Lord Mayor's Show, and its miniature winter season of entertainments and assemblies.

There were comparable services and diversions for county society in the other provincial capitals, exemplified by the fashionable quarter of St. Augustine's and the coffee-houses of late seventeenth-century Bristol, or by the New London Inn, 'the great inn of the county community', at Exeter. Only Newcastle, faced with competition from the Palatine capital of Durham, could not claim a similar success. But its wealth could not be ignored by the rural élite and like other regional centres it served as an important money-market. By the seventeenth century the merchants of the town were 'bankers for the whole of North England from the Tweed to the Tees.' Exeter too was a vital source of mortgages and credit for the surrounding countryside as well as a centre for dealings in bills of exchange. Exeter indeed combined all the functions of a provincial capital. According to Defoe, it was 'a city famous for two things, which we seldom find unite in the same town, (viz.) that 'tis full of gentry and good company, and yet full of trade and manufactures also.'

Given their size and long-term economic resilience it is not surprising that, like some of the more successful county towns, all the provincial capitals displayed a rich panoply of civic and economic institutions which allowed the mercantile élite to dominate and control their affairs. Their governing charters had established self-perpetuating oligarchic councils by the beginning of the sixteenth century and these steadily engrossed authority at the expense of the theoretically enfranchised freemen. Norwich and York had two councils, one more responsive to freeman opinion than the other: even so the twenty-four aldermen of the Norwich Court increasingly took decisions which the sixty common councillors merely rubber-stamped, while in York almost all effective power lay with the inner aldermanic élite. In Newcastle, Bristol, and Exeter there were single councils including the aldermen, but by the seventeenth century the mayor and aldermen of Bristol were meeting separately for detailed discussion of business, and the Exeter Chamber of Twenty-Four was itself a small, closed oligarchy from 1509. Like other towns, the provincial capitals also possessed numerous gilds and craft companies, from the sixty-four in York in 1579 to the fourteen in Exeter by 1586. But for most of our period they were under the direct control of municipal councils. Thus at Norwich in 1622 the trades were amalgamated into twelve great companies which enabled the larger crafts to dominate and control the smaller. Only the major organizations like the Merchant Adventurers, all separately chartered by the Crown, had any real autonomy, and they were invariably closely identified with the ruling oligarchy.

Political life was shaped, therefore, by a small group of powerful and wealthy men. The exceptions were few and excited comment, like John Woolcott, elected mayor of Exeter in 1565, who was of 'small wealth' though once a great merchant: according to Hooker, 'it was not thought nor meant that ever the office of the mayoralty should have fallen unto his lot'. Generally the rulers were men whose wealth was based on trade, international or internal, who were purchasing lands in the countryside, but who also had interests in the other economic activities of the provincial capitals. A typical Exeter example was Thomas Richardson, mayor in

1566, who 'kept a wine tavern and was a merchant adven-
turer . . . and did not only serve this city by retail but also all
the gentlemen in the shire of Devon by the tuns and
hogsheads.'

The political problems caused by the rule of these élites
will be considered in detail in chapter nine. Attacks on the
oligarchy were certainly frequent and sometimes violent.
There were disturbances in Exeter, Newcastle, and York in
the first two decades of the sixteenth century. Peasant revolts
and rural disturbances might also join forces with the urban
commonalty to threaten the oligarchy, as in York at the time
of the Pilgrimage of Grace and in Norwich during Ket's
rebellion. Even Bristol felt the effects in 1549: there was 'a
great insurrection . . . and many young men plucked up
hedges . . . which enclosed grounds near the city and after-
wards rebelled against the mayor, so that he and all his
brethren with him were forced to go into the marsh with
weapons.' As in other towns, however, oligarchic rule was not
significantly disturbed either by Tudor disorder or, more
surprisingly, by the political conflicts of the following century.

Politically, the provincial capitals were set apart from
country towns by their relative independence of outside
authorities. All had their own quarter sessions and justices
of the peace, and, with the exception of Exeter, which was
granted the privilege only in 1537, all had been county
boroughs since the early fifteenth century. Like other provincial towns, of course, they needed patrons at Court, and
they were always the junior partners in their relations with
the Crown and its agents. Bristol chose Thomas Cromwell as
its Recorder in 1533 and regularly elected Privy Councillors
as High Steward. It also had to fight a prolonged battle to
resist the jurisdictional claims over the town of the Council in
the Marches of Wales. The Council in the North had real
authority over the York corporation, even summoning the
mayor before it in 1541 to answer complaints made against
him by the parishioners of Holy Trinity, Goodramgate. On
the other hand, the provincial capitals were powerful and
influential enough to be able to reduce the numerous local
liberties which limited their municipal jurisdiction; Bristol

obtaining the franchises of St. Augustine and Temple at the Reformation and the Castle in 1629. They were also unusual in their ability to resist political pressure from the local nobility. For most of our period they regularly chose their own citizens as M.P.s. Thus Exeter rebuffed the nominees of the Earl of Bedford in 1562, and only two or three of Newcastle's M.P.s between 1559 and 1831 had no immediate close connection with the town. The only major exception was later Stuart York: here political divisions in town and county and the Crown's attack on corporation charters pushed a less confident council into choosing country gentlemen as its representatives.

If the size and wealth of these cities gave them an unusual political sophistication and resilience, they needed both to deal with the social problems which growth and economic change brought with them. Their problems, both short- and long-term, were those of other towns writ large. There were fires, like the major disaster at Norwich in 1507 in which 1,718 houses were said to have been burnt in four days. There were periodic food crises and plagues; the worst occurred in Norwich in 1579 and Newcastle in 1636. While our evidence suggests that the economies of the provincial capitals quickly recovered after such crises, other problems were more persistent. With their high death rates these cities were even more heavily dependent on immigration than smaller towns, and their attraction for migrants of all kinds extended over unusually large areas. Bristol's apprentices came from most counties up the Severn; and even Newcastle, with a more limited area of recruitment, drew young men and women from all four northern counties. In towns of this size large numbers of apprentices might well pose formidable problems to public order: they rioted in Newcastle in 1633 and took temporary control of Bristol in 1660. But immigrants of lower social status, paupers and vagrants, increasingly occupied the energies of constables and courts in each city and aggravated their most pressing problem, that of poverty.

When the town clerk of Norwich declared in 1670 that 'poverty daily invades us like an armed man' he was articulating the experience shared by his predecessors for more

than a century. In the same town a census taken in 1570 had
found that nearly a quarter of the non-alien population was
in some sense poor. This was at the height of the depression
in the textile industry which had produced complaints of the
'daily increase' in destitution in other provincial capitals.
Poverty was endemic in these towns for most of our period;
it was also made particularly obvious by the unusually clear
topographical segregation of rich and poor. The Hearth
Taxes of the 1660s show that each large town had a small
central nucleus of rich parishes, full of large merchants'
houses and shops, and much poorer districts on their
boundaries packed with the one- or two-room hovels of
labourers. The poorest area of Exeter, for instance, was the
growing suburb of St. Sidwell's; the slums of Newcastle were
in Sandgate, east of the walls, populated largely by keelmen
and colliers. In such towns the class structure was visible on
the ground.

None of the corporations could hope to do more than
mitigate some of the worst symptoms presented by the
poverty of large fractions of their populations. But their
citizens' pockets and corporate finances were better able to
bear the financial burden of supporting the poor than were
those of smaller towns, and it was a mark of their administrative sophistication as well as of the scale of the problem,
that some of the provincial capitals were national innovators
in the provision of poor relief. They all enjoyed rich charitable endowments, like the benefaction of Sir Thomas White
in 1566 which Bristol controlled and whose benefits were
shared by twenty-four other towns, including the other
provincial capitals. They successfully fought to retain their
medieval hospitals at the Dissolution and attracted new
foundations. Exeter had nine sets of almshouses by 1640; York
at least twelve by the end of the century. But the corporations
also invested a large proportion of their time and capital in
inaugurating compulsory poor rates, censuses of the poor,
workhouses, and employment schemes, which formed the
models for national legislation and which were copied and
admired in other towns.

This was only one of the ways in which provincial capitals

influenced their neighbours. In other respects their impact beyond their walls was similar to that of lesser county towns, though it extended further and probably persisted longer. They were important centres for education after the Reformation, with their endowed grammar schools, the cathedral schools at York and Exeter, and new schools for poor children modelled on Christ's Hospital in Exeter and Bristol. Exeter's Latin cathedral school alone had 200 students by 1630. The educational ideals of these corporations were also expressed in the free town libraries founded in Norwich in 1608 and Bristol in 1613, and in proposals for universities in York in the 1640s and in Durham in the 1650s (the latter supported by Newcastle's aldermen). There was even a partial revival of local printing and publishing to add to the cultural influence of York, Newcastle, and Bristol at the end of the seventeenth century.

The provincial capitals also exercised an important influence as religious centres, but only after they had first recovered from the destructive changes wrought by the Reformation. The 1530s saw their religious houses disappear, five of them in Exeter, twice as many in York (including the richest monastery in the North, St. Mary's Abbey). At the same time, the physical expression of the religious identity of the community was attenuated by the amalgamation of parishes, by the destruction of chantries, and the abolition of religious gilds. However, the provincial capitals gradually became leading regional centres first for Protestantism— some of the earliest disturbances of the Reformation occurred at Bristol and Exeter in the 1530s—and later for Puritanism and Dissent. This development was encouraged by corporate support for town lectureships, like those in Exeter in 1600 and Bristol in 1607, by powerful preachers like Henry Aiscough of York and Robert Jenison of Newcastle in the early seventeenth century, and by the determined activity of urban parishioners themselves, winning, for example, the right to present to benefices, as they had done in five Norwich parishes before 1600. Already in the 1580s Norwich, with its ministers and magistrates united in opposition to Bishop Freake, was one of the leading Puritan centres in the kingdom, and by the early seventeenth century the other towns contained Puritan aldermen, like Ignatius Jurdain of Exeter, determined to create similar godly commonwealths.

After 1640 the religious influence of these towns persisted, but in less coherent and more fragmented form. Bristol, for example, became a centre for the religious sects, its Baptist church at Broadmead having close connections with sectarianism in South Wales and London. By the 1680s there were also Presbyterian, Independent, and Quaker congregations in the city, while the Baptists were in close correspondence with neighbouring congregations in Taunton and Chipping Sodbury. Exeter and Newcastle had achieved a similar influence over Nonconformity in Devon and the North by that date, and even York, with its influential ecclesiastical establishment, had several Dissenting congregations and was already a centre for Yorkshire Quakers. The provincial capitals retained some of their religious power, along with other aspects of their regional influence.

The civic identity of the provincial capital, as perceived by its citizens, had undeniably changed in the course of our period. Its religious processions had disappeared soon after the Reformation. Many of the great ecclesiastical buildings which overshadowed its townscape had gone. Public building now took a more secular form and bore witness to the dominant concerns of particular groups rather than those of the community as a whole. There were new council-houses for the oligarchies of Exeter in the 1590s and Newcastle in the 1650s; at York impressive extensions were added to the King's Manor for the Council in the North; and in each town there were new almshouses and hospitals. But private building, new or improved houses for merchants and gentlemen, a few new housing developments like those in the Castle precinct of Bristol in the 1650s, the growth of suburbs in Exeter and Newcastle, did more to alter the physical appearance of these cities. Nevertheless, their image had probably changed less than that of many other towns. If by 1700 they had lost many of the formal expressions of their older identity as religious and civic communities, they at least retained their walls as reminders of their independence and the bustle of their streets, inns, and markets as testimony to their continued wealth and regional impact.

Like other towns in this period, the provincial capitals had experienced serious problems, particularly in their economic and social sectors. As we have seen, they had had to adjust to changes in their industrial and commercial functions and they had been faced with the social stresses caused by growth and change. The Reformation had destroyed much of their cultural individuality and the influence of country gentlemen increasingly dominated their social life by the end of our period. Yet compared with many lesser centres the provincial capitals had survived relatively unscathed: in 1700 they were all large and prosperous towns. The citizens of Bristol could still take pride in the number and size of ships at the regularly repaired quays; those of York in the splendid Elizabethan bridge over the Ouse with its shops, council-house, and heavy traffic. Even so, by the end of the seventeenth century one can detect a shift of direction and orientation. When visitors complimented Newcastle, York or Norwich it was usually less on account of their independent status and influence as representatives of the provinces, than on their new resemblance to London. The metropolis had become the exemplar and the mentor of English urban society.

5

London

PRECEDING chapters have already indicated the growing importance of London between 1500 and 1700. In fact the growth of the metropolis was the most spectacular development in English urban society in the period. James I commented, at the start of the seventeenth century, that London would soon devour all England and a century later John Strype hailed the city as the 'glory of the kingdom'. International recognition was forthcoming too: the Italian, Giovanni Botero, declared in 1588 that London was the only city in England that 'deserves to be called great'. By 1700 the metropolis—the old walled city plus the satellite communities of Westminster, Southwark, and East London—was already the largest city in Western Europe with a population of over half a million. Throughout the two centuries under survey, the capital stood in an urban class of its own; and the differences between it and other English towns increased rather than diminished with time.

It is important, however, to put London's rise into perspective. We should not forget that even during the Middle Ages London had been the undisputed champion of the urban league table, with a population three times as great as those of its nearest rivals, Bristol and York. It had also enjoyed a European reputation as a major city on a par with Cologne or Ghent. The foundations of London's medieval importance were many. One was its central trading role astride the main internal lines of communication; another was its strategic position as a port, located on the largest river, and having close ties with Germany, the Low Countries, France, and Italy; a third was its industrial function, producing specialist and semi-luxury goods. Finally, there was its close proximity to the main seat of government and the royal courts at Westminster. This not only attracted to the city the custom and residence of county landowners, but thrust it into political prominence, a prominence leading to its establishment after 1327 as a full-fledged, urban community with its own highly-developed civic constitution. This striking diversity of function was undoubtedly the great strength of the capital and enabled it to withstand the many problems of the later medieval economy. The same functional heterogeneity also provided the essential springboard for the city's take-off in the sixteenth and seventeenth centuries.

The most obvious aspect of metropolitan growth after 1500 was demographic. It seems probable that the number of inhabitants within the city walls and in the suburbs under city control rose from about 40,000 at the start of the sixteenth century to 300,000 in 1700; the rate of increase was greatest outside the walls. Even faster expansion occurred in the areas beyond the city limits, in Whitechapel, Stepney, and Shadwell to the east, and Westminster to the west. By 1700 these areas had a population totalling more than 200,000. In 1550 the districts east of the city were still mostly rural with only pockets of industrial and urban development; one hundred and fifty years later there was high-density, lower-class housing there and also important textile and ship-building activity. At about that time Strype declared that East London was 'furnished with everything that may entitle it to the honour ... of a great town'. With the poor and artisan classes increasingly concentrated in the eastern suburbs of the metropolis, the wealthy pushed to the west, encouraged by the fashionable proximity of the Court. The Earl of Bedford's development of Covent Garden and William Newton's grand new houses in Queen's Street, both in the 1630s, set the pattern for a wave of splendid squares and mansions for the landed élite, successful city financiers, and courtiers. Luxury traders like goldsmiths, anxious to keep their clientele, dutifully followed them west.

The rate of London's demographic growth was all the more dramatic because little or none of it was due to natural

increase. Admittedly, there may have been some surplus of
baptisms over burials in the less urbanized parts of Elizabethan East London, but by the next century burial rates
held the upper hand in most parishes. Overcrowding plus
inadequate sanitation, occasional periods of food-shortage,
endemic and epidemic disease all contributed to the high
mortality rates, especially among infants and children.
Bubonic plague, in particular, regularly decimated the city's
population. In 1603 alone more than 40,000 people died,
perhaps a fifth of the inhabitants—most from the suburbs
outside the city walls: 2,879 in St. Giles' Cripplegate, 2,228 in
Stepney. The plague of 1563 had been still more severe. But
no less serious, if less spectacular, were the recurrent attacks of
influenza, typhus, and smallpox which afflicted the metropolis up to 1700.

In order to fill its ranks the city recruited heavily from the
provinces. Long distance migration to the capital was
already well established in the early fourteenth century, with
a significant influx from East Anglia and the North. The
principal change in the sixteenth and seventeenth centuries
was in the type and scale of immigration. Whereas medieval
migration usually involved respectable people becoming
apprentices in the city gilds, many immigrants between 1500
and 1700 were the poor and destitute, who journeyed to
London in desperate hope of casual work or charity, and who
crowded the small tenements of the poor parishes or squatted
in suburban slums. They probably formed the bulk of the
8,000 or so net immigrants whom late Stuart London
absorbed every year. Many were young and single; a high
proportion were women, not a few perhaps like Jane Crooke
of Oxford, whose lover sent her to the capital 'until that she
had been delivered' of his child. Some failed to find housing
or work: in the early seventeenth century 1,000 vagrants were
being admitted to Bridewell every year. But many were
packed into overcrowded lodgings and thus contributed to
the heavy incidence of disease and death. In 1614 one
Westminster landlord housed six men and women in one
small room.

However, one must not forget the substantial minority of

more traditional immigrants who came to take up apprenticeships, hoping to rise to be freemen, masters, and even
perhaps gild wardens. Entrance to the great companies, like
the Grocers, was difficult for all but the children of prosperous countryfolk, though it was not a monopoly of the
landed gentry. But the multitude of smaller crafts provided a
reasonable hope of success for those with lesser (albeit
respectable) backgrounds. Thus, one John Browne claimed
in 1631 that he had worked in Leicester years before dressing
hemp but had not been able to make a living; 'but now since
my coming from thence up to London I am a freeman of the
city and of the company of merchant tailors', profitably
self-employed. Significantly, it was towards the close of the
sixteenth century that the story of Dick Whittington was first
recorded in city and national folk-lore. According to one
recent estimate, there may have been as many as 20,000
apprentices in the capital in the mid-seventeenth century,
with up to 40 per cent of them coming from the North and
the Midlands.

As in the Middle Ages, foreign trade was one of the more
notable and eye-catching sectors of the city's business life.
By the early Tudor period the London Merchant Adventurers controlled the lion's share of England's main export
trade, that in unfinished cloth sold to the Netherlands and
northern Germany. While the trade experienced cyclical and
other more extended crises, mainly owing to war, it was
generally profitable throughout the sixteenth century. By
the early decades of the seventeenth, however, the dominant
position of the Merchant Adventurers was being challenged,
mainly by a combination of East India and Levant Company
merchants, the latter exporting the cheaper, finished, new
draperies to the Mediterranean. In turn their leading role in
the mercantile community came under attack after 1640 from
a powerful group of interlopers and other merchants involved
in the colonial trades. Much of their business involved re-
exports (amounting by 1699–1701 to a third of all English
exports), and London soon overtook Amsterdam as the
principal entrepôt in Western Europe. Here London's long-
established shipping ties with the continent knitted together

with the port's growing network of extra-European commerce, the latter now dominated by the great joint-stock companies such as the East India and Royal African Companies.

Yet it would be wrong to account for London's economic success primarily in terms of its role as the capital of the 'Commercial Revolution' of the seventeenth century. Out of a sample of 140 London aldermen in the early Stuart period, about half were engaged in domestic trade, dealing in provincial cloths, imported cloths, and general wholesale goods, while even in the late seventeenth century the majority of great merchants whose estates are registered in the London Court of Orphans were not primarily export merchants. The importance of the domestic trades in London's economy was nothing new. Already in the late Middle Ages London merchants had established a network of trading connections across the Home Counties: hence, for example, the metropolitan grain trade with East Kent. But now this network was consolidated and extended to cover a large sector of the kingdom. Thus, by the end of the sixteenth century, London merchants like Sir George Bolles were busy supplying Northern consumers with general wares and commodities, mainly through Hull. In exchange for the imported and specialist goods which city traders distributed to market-towns and countryside, the provinces were harnessed to victual the metropolis: imports of grain alone rose from 68,596 quarters in 1615 to 191,650 quarters in 1680–1. The seventeenth century saw the inauguration of sixteen new markets in the suburbs to cope with the influx of grain and livestock. Indeed, without this constantly growing supply of foodstuffs, it is questionable whether the capital could have expanded at such a startling rate. As one observer noted, "tis hard to know which is the most to be admired at, the prodigious number of the inhabitants . . . or the vast plenty . . . of provisions wherewith they are supplied.'

Fundamental to the orientation of internal trade towards London was the development of domestic transport. An important and probably growing proportion of London's provincial commerce was carted overland. Thus the number of carriers operating out of the capital may well have trebled between 1637 and 1715. But the great bulk of the capital's domestic trade was transported more cheaply by river and coastal shipping. In the early eighteenth century London had as many as nineteen major quays specializing in various branches of provincial traffic: Queenhithe, according to Strype, was 'much resorted to by barges and lighters, which bring up goods from the western parts of the kingdom as corn, wood etc . . .'. Domestic water-borne trade gave the metropolitan port an essential resilience which allowed it to ride out the more violent troughs of foreign commerce. No wonder Sir Josiah Child declared in 1694: 'I cannot myself remember since there were not in London used so many wharves and quays for the lading of merchants' goods.' By then about a quarter of the city's population may have been engaged in port work.

Closely related to the growth of the port was the development of several major industries. Shipbuilding was the most obvious, with several large and many small shipyards springing up along the Thames at Blackwall, Wapping, and Ratcliffe. The new colonial trades also led to the establishment of large sugar refineries in East London. At the same time, older luxury trades like that of the goldsmiths continued to flourish, while the influx of Huguenot textile workers made the Spitalfields silk industry a major rival to the French. The building industry in general had a field-day with many small-scale developments in the East End and to the north of the city, as well as the grand estates in Piccadilly, St. James's and Bloomsbury. The only industries which seem to have suffered were those, like metal-work and clothing, which faced increasingly successful competition by the later seventeenth century from new provincial manufacturers, benefiting from lower wage rates and larger units of production. In 1675 there were serious riots by weavers, aimed at preventing the reorganization of the London industry on a more competitive footing.

Another growth sector in London's highly variegated economy was service activities. Though an established feature of the medieval city, there can be little question that the service sector grew rapidly during our period. Since the metropolis housed not only the headquarters of the legal profession, the Inns of Court, but also the chief royal courts, it is hardly surprising that legal services were especially prominent. They took advantage of an astonishing expansion in legal business: the number of pleas entered in King's Bench rose tenfold during the sixteenth century, while the number of suits initiated in Chancery jumped from 200 a year in the 1560s to 500 a year in the 1590s. Parallel to this the number of enrolled attorneys in the Court of Common Pleas increased from 342 to 1,383 between 1578 and 1633. It is true that not all the cases were heard in London (a substantial proportion were eventually tried at assizes), while some of the enrolled attorneys concentrated on provincial practice. Nonetheless, for most of our period, the London lawyers and all the ancillary trades profited tremendously. Other professions also made hay while the metropolitan sun shone. By 1704 there were said to be as many as 1,000 London apothecaries, and their numbers may well have multiplied tenfold since 1500. The Stuart city was also famous for its astrologers, men like William Lilly, for its physicians, scriveners, bookbinders, and schoolmasters. As we shall see, London was a principal beneficiary of the 'Educational Revolution'.

The service sector brought to the metropolis both the business and the physical presence of many provincial men. In the sixteenth century a growing number of county grandees owned or rented a house in the capital; in the next century a stay in London during the 'season' became a social necessity for any major landowner who wanted to hold his head high in provincial society. By 1700 a significant number were purchasing property in the new squares west of Charing Cross. Their presence and their landed revenues contributed heavily to London's growth as a centre of conspicuous consumption and as the capital of high fashion. During the 1680s more than 30 per cent of the Verneys' income from their Claydon rents was being transferred to London, and in the case of the Fitzwilliam family's income in Northampton-shire the figure may have been as high as 77 per cent between 1696 and 1700.

The development of the West End for the nation's ruling élite underlined the great extremes of wealth and the growing social segregation within greater London. Complementing the great households with their income of three thousand pounds a year or more were the migrant labourers and seamen concentrated in the East End, living on a few shillings a month. The economic pyramid was equally acute and stratified in the business community of the city proper. R. B. Grassby's work on the personal estates of city freemen has suggested that only about 5 per cent of those dying in the period 1678–93 had more than £5,000: among the tycoons were Sir John Banks and Sir Josiah Child who both left over £100,000. Below this narrow élite was a somewhat broader group of freemen in the £1,000–£5,000 bracket; this would have been enough to put them at the top of the merchant élite in most provincial towns. At the lower end of the spectrum were many small citizens, with less than £100. Further down still were the great tribes of artisans and journeymen who overlapped with the suburban poor. These sharp differences in wealth were also mirrored in residential differentiation within the city. If the level of philanthropic activity is any guide, the areas with the wealthiest inhabitants were the central parishes like St. Olave Jewry and St. Mary Aldermary, close to the Guildhall and the Exchange, while the poorer parishes tended to be near the riverside or close to the walls, spilling over into the suburbs outside Aldgate and Bishopsgate.

Social tension and discontent were obvious consequences of this economic and social polarization. Food riots, often led by apprentices, recurred throughout the sixteenth century and were a constant cause of government concern. There were also sporadic attacks on aliens, the most famous in 1517. But the principal area of conflict was the gilds. Tudor London, like most provincial towns, witnessed a concerted effort by greater merchants and traders to tighten their hold over the city's ninety or so craft companies. By the 1560s, for example, a small inner ring can be seen in control of the Salters Company, the precursor of an oligarchic court of assistants. Gild conflict was often three-cornered, with small masters frequently, though not invariably, uniting with the apprentices and journeymen against the magnates. Feuding was particularly serious during the 1640s when economic instability, caused by civil war and harvest failure, pushed small masters and their servants into violent agitation. Since the gild structure was closely integrated with the municipal government of the city, conflict within the crafts inevitably led to disputes and disorder within the corporation. In 1641 the oligarchic power of the aldermen, most of them great merchants and financiers, was sharply curtailed by a coalition of middle and lesser merchants and masters. Later in the 1640s combinations of masters, apprentices, and journeymen struggled further to liberalize civic and gild politics, though with only limited success in 1648 and 1649.

Agitation in the city during the 1640s had important implications for national politics. The successful overthrow of the pro-royalist, aldermanic clique in 1641 ensured the city's support for the more radical faction in the Long Parliament and its determination to confront the King. In 1647 and 1648 the populist Leveller movement in the capital joined forces with the left wing of the New Model Army to challenge, or so it seemed, the established social order of the nation. Again, during the Exclusion Crisis of 1678–81, the middling and small merchants and traders of the city threw their weight behind the parliamentary attack on Charles II and his Catholic brother, the Duke of York. It was a mark of London's unique position on the English urban scene that it had a leading role in national politics, a role which continued into the eighteenth century.

The political importance of the metropolis was in part simply a consequence of the city's size and its close proximity to central government and Parliament. But it also reflected a wide range of other variables. Not least important was the growing wealth of its mercantile community. From the 1570s English governments relied on large city loans to finance much of their day-to-day activities; in the 1690s this relationship was embodied in the Bank of England. In consequence, ministers tried to build up a loyal following in the city, usually from among the great merchants. This in turn exacerbated the political strains within the government of the city and gilds which, as we have seen, were the mainspring of radical agitation during the seventeenth century. Another factor affecting London's political prominence was the administrative weakness of the corporation. By the seventeenth century the metropolis had outgrown the administrative and police organization centred on the old city. The city fathers had made no attempt to extend their jurisdiction to cover the new suburbs to the north, east, and west. As a result, much of greater London was ruled by an impotent alliance of parish, manorial, and county authorities. Unlike the rest of the kingdom, where the seventeenth century saw the landed élite tightening its political control over the county communities, the government of outer London steadily disintegrated, making it vulnerable to political agitation. Finally, London's importance in national politics, particularly radical politics, was powerfully enhanced by the city's role as the country's leading centre of new ideas and attitudes.

Prior to the Reformation the city's cultural life had been dominated by the Church. As well as St. Paul's, the capital possessed more than one hundred parish churches and a multitude of religious houses mainly clustered outside its walls. The craft gilds, usually associated with particular parish churches, also had a religious bias, supporting chantries and processions as well as feast-days. However, with the Reformation, the dense undergrowth of civic religion was cleared. The gilds lost their religious associations and civic ceremony was secularized. The famous Lord Mayor's Show (29 October) supplanted the quasi-religious pageants of the gilds at Midsummer. By James I's reign it was highly theatrical, choreographed by leading dramatists like Thomas Dekker and Thomas Middleton, and directed less at the citizenry than at the smart gentlemen from the Court and country.

Nonetheless, religion remained a powerful force in the city. Already before the Reformation London had been a vital centre of new theological ideas, imported from the continent. Thereafter it showed a firm commitment to radical theology.

The famous pulpit in St. Paul's churchyard attracted all the established preachers in the kingdom. Less orthodox, but no less popular, were the Puritan lectureships which sprang up in every parish to supplement the religious services of the ordinary clergy: by the 1630s, 107 London parishes employed active lecturers. The most radical often ministered in the suburbs or in the religious liberties which lay outside diocesan control: the well-known William Gouge preached at St. Anne's, Blackfriars, and was regularly heard by a large congregation of substantial tradesmen and provincial godly. Nor was London's wider religious impact confined to those countrymen who journeyed to the city. Throughout the late sixteenth and early seventeenth centuries, city merchants and lawyers endowed a wide range of provincial lectureships, worth about £20,000. From the 1620s individual practice was put on a formal collective footing with the creation of the Feoffees for Impropriations, who gradually acquired the patronage of livings scattered over eighteen counties. Testimony to their success came from Archbishop Laud who declared that they sought 'to overthrow the church government by getting to their power more dependency of the clergy than the king and all the peers and all the bishops in all the kingdom had.' The government suppressed the Feoffees in 1633.

Extremist religious sects also found a home in the metropolis. The early separatists drew much of their support from economically depressed minor tradesmen and shipworkers living mainly in the suburbs. From 1621 there was an active Baptist conventicle in Southwark near St. Mary Overy's church, and in 1638 a separatist congregation of weavers, cordwainers, and sailors was meeting in Rotherhithe. The same kind of folk filled the ranks of the Fifth Monarchists and the Quakers. The former had numerous congregations in the capital, including those at Blackfriars (under Christopher Feake), Swan Alley, Coleman Street, and Southwark. In 1654 the Quaker, George Fox, visited London and 'had great and powerful meetings: so great were the throngs of people that I could hardly get to and from the meetings for the crowds of people: and the truth spread significantly.' In 1655

the Quakers took over a meeting-place house in Aldersgate
with standing room for a thousand. However, the failure of
the Revolution, the demoralization and fragmentation of the
sects, and the growing importance in London after 1660 of
the county grandees made the metropolis less influential as a
centre of militant Puritanism. The resurgence of evangelical
Christianity in the eighteenth century was primarily a provincial phenomenon.

The role of the metropolis as an important centre of
education was more continuous. Already influential at the
start of our period, London became a dynamic force in the
subsequent educational expansion. Colet's St. Paul's School
was the model for a whole series of provincial endowments,
while Westminster School (reorganized in 1560) and the
Merchant Taylors' School (1561) were among the foremost
educational establishments in the kingdom, Westminster, in
particular, attracting numerous pupils from the provinces.
The sixteenth century also saw the foundation of a host of
smaller grammar schools in and about the city. Not surprisingly, there was a high level of metropolitan literacy. By
the early seventeenth century only 24 per cent of a sample of
city tradesmen and artisans were unable to sign their names.
The minds of the citizenry were further improved by public
lectures at Surgeons' Hall, the College of Physicians, and
Gresham College, where the subjects dealt with included
astronomy, geometry, physic, and law. The Inns of Court,
now aspiring to become the third university of the kingdom,
catered mainly for the sons of country gentry and lawyers.
London's educational influence was also enlarged through
philanthropy. Between 1480 and 1660 nearly £200,000 was
donated by Londoners for educational purposes in the provinces, with at least half expended in the backward and
conservative areas of the highland zone. After the middle of
the seventeenth century, however, there was a shift in emphasis. Some of the city's smaller grammar schools began
to decline and growth in the established centres for adult
education, like the Inns of Court, had stopped. Expansion
was now confined to the leading endowed schools (like
Westminster) and academies for the offspring of the landed

aristocracy come to town. The academies were usually located in the more fashionable suburbs: in the 1680s, for example, we hear of Monsieur Foubert who 'has set up an academy near the Haymarket for riding, fencing, dancing, handling arms and mathematics.'

Other facets of the city's cultural image also reveal the growing influence of the aristocratic encampment in the West End. The melodramas, tragedies, and comic satires of the Elizabethan and Jacobean stage, many of whose themes appealed to citizen taste, gave way after the Restoration to more sophisticated comedies with their stress on romance, wit, and intrigue in high society. Like the fashionable academies, they owed a good deal to French influence, and they reflected London's role as the cosmopolitan arbiter of upper-class taste. Even the prevailing fashions in public drinking and social intercourse changed. From the 1650s the old respectable drinking establishments, inns and taverns, faced competition from new houses selling cocoa, tea, and above all coffee. By the early eighteenth century there were over 500 coffee-houses in the capital. One ingredient in their success was the rise of the Levant trades in the city (Turkish baths were also fashionable); but no less important was the social pressure for more exclusive meeting places for the greater merchants and landed classes. Here the élite might talk business and politics, and read the latest newspapers: in the 1690s there was a standard arrangement for newspapers to be on sale at well-patronized coffee-houses.

Newspapers were one of the more exciting manifestations of London's cultural effervescence at the end of our period. By 1712 as many as twenty single-leaf papers were being published each week in the city; three years later the author of the *British Mercury* claimed that 'near 4,000 [were] printed every time, and those carefully distributed into all parts, not only of this city, but of the whole nation.' Since the few provincial papers operating at this time mostly reprinted London copy, the capital had a virtual monopoly of the news media. In fact, its control over the printed word was much older. In 1558 the Crown, determined to tighten censorship, had closed down the small provincial presses and concentrated professional publishing in the hands of the London Stationers Company. Though production rose sharply before 1640, almost doubling in Elizabeth's reign alone, the monopoly held up surprisingly well. Even during the 1640s, when official censorship collapsed, almost all printing was still done in London: in 1645 over 700 newspapers, most of them short-lived, were printed there. When the licensing controls finally lapsed in the 1690s the capital enjoyed an impregnable position. This control over the media was fundamental to the increasing influence, if not dominance, of metropolitan values and attitudes over provincial respectability evident by 1700.

All this would suggest that London's demographic explosion was only one aspect of metropolitan growth and change between 1500 and 1700. How do we account for the phenomenon? Earlier we stressed the diversity of London's mixed economy at the end of the Middle Ages, putting it in a stronger position than most of its provincial competitors. But other factors were equally important. Some we have already mentioned in preceding chapters; others were peculiar to London. National population growth was particularly important in the sixteenth century. It helped to determine the movement of migrants into towns; it also produced rapid inflation in the prices of foodstuffs, which provided larger incomes for the farming community and, through rising rents, for the landed classes. This had many profitable repercussions for the capital: increased expenditure on litigation at the Westminster courts, more visits by the gentry and, above all, an increasing provincial demand for fashionable commodities, both native and imported.

London was especially well-placed to satisfy the demands generated by the growth of conspicuous consumption. In addition to its long-established trading ties with the provinces, the city's own needs made it an ideal partner in internal trade. Profits from London's sales in the countryside were used to pay for the cereals and other commodities essential to provision its soaring population. This, in turn, gave a further boost to agricultural prices and landed prosperity. No less important was the advantage London enjoyed as the country's pre-eminent international port. In the sixteenth century the overseas trade of the capital depended heavily on exports, but during the next century the bias was turned towards imports, partly in response to provincial demand.

There can be little question that in the late seventeenth century the import trade was a leading source of London's prosperity and growth in its own right. By then provincial demand was less crucial, for the country's population and grain prices were relatively static and provincial prosperity was more limited and selective. What was now vital was the city's ability (backed by the Navigation Acts) to exploit the Dutch and French entanglement in continental wars in order to take the lead in the international distribution of mainly colonial goods. Trade, thus, gave London a paramount economic role in Europe as well as in England.

Politics were also closely involved in metropolitan growth. The rising number of lawsuits heard in Westminster Hall owed much to the decline of local courts in the face of the growing power of new royal courts like Star Chamber and Requests. Increased royal intervention in the provinces also led to bureaucratic expansion in the capital, particularly during the 1530s and 1540s with the establishment of the Courts of Augmentations and Wards. Not less significantly, the seventeenth century saw both the Court and Parliament functioning on an increasingly regular basis in the metropolis. As a result, London became a cockpit for the pursuit of office and party intrigue, luring to the West End the great magnates who by now dominated provincial England.

So far in this chapter we have sought to describe and to explain metropolitan growth between 1500 and 1700. In conclusion we must try to assess the significance of that growth, both in terms of its general impact on the nation and of the kind of urban society which it created.

Recent studies have tended to emphasize the positive implications of London's rise, particularly for the provincial economy. Metropolitan expansion has been seen as giving a major boost to internal trade and to agricultural specialization and production. However, as we have already noted, London was for much of our period less the originator of economic change than the mediator of developments based essentially in the provinces themselves, such as the growth of population and of landed incomes. Moreover, whatever the cause, the consequences of the increasing dominance of the capital were hardly greeted with rapturous provincial applause. Reaction was almost always hostile. In 1596, for instance, the merchants of Hull complained that London traders had established their agents at nearby Gainsborough 'to whom they send such store of foreign [wares] to serve the country, that they have drawn away almost all the trade from the aforesaid port.' Already deprived of much of their overseas trade by London merchants, the provincial ports were increasingly threatened by metropolitan encroachments on their coastal traffic: hence the particular bitterness of the confrontation between London and the outports in James I's reign.

Local merchants were not the only critics of the capital's increased activity in the provincial economy. Since the diversion of food supplies to the capital occurred without any major improvements in agricultural production, at least before the early seventeenth century, the benefits which accrued to the landed and farming interests from higher prices and higher rents hardly compensated for the deteriorating living standards of the lower orders. At Chelmsford in 1631 it was said that 'the chandlers of London haunt all the market near unto London and sweep the market of all the corn that comes'. Food riots were recurrent and widespread throughout the areas which supplied the capital. In bad harvest years provincial towns were sometimes forced to import cereals from the continent to make up local food deficiencies caused by the transport of grain to London. No wonder many poorer folk saw migration to the capital as their only hope.

Prior to 1640 it is difficult to avoid the impression that London's exceptional growth was mainly parasitical, feeding off the significant redistribution of wealth which was occurring in the provincial economy. Admittedly there were probably some consequent improvements in the organization of internal trade. Coastal and river shipping expanded while the services of provincial carriers out of London more than doubled during the seventeenth century. Again, the growing demands of the London food market stimulated agricultural specialization in the south-east: corn-growing in Cambridge-shire, dairy-farming in Suffolk, cattle-fattening in Essex and Buckinghamshire, market-gardening closer to the capital, (Battersea was famous for its asparagus). But it is often very difficult to disentangle the contribution of London itself from the influence of national demographic trends and the chang-ing patterns of demand in the country as a whole. In the economic field we can certainly see some parallels between London and the modern, rapidly expanding cities of the Third World, which in a number of respects, retard rather than assist real economic growth. The problem is too complex to consider fully here, but it may be significant that, as with the present-day cities of south-east Asia, London's commercial success in the sixteenth century relied heavily on cannibalizing the trade of provincial ports, while much of its growing population was underemployed and could only be supported by an unhealthy expansion of marginal, service activities. For less ambiguous evidence of the positive impact of London before 1640 we have to turn away from the economy: to politics, where London's courts and other institutions were principal agents of growing national unity and cohesion; to the social arena, where London fashions set national stan-dards among the ruling élite; and to the realm of ideas, where London Puritanism took the lead in a modernizing war on the ignorance, illiteracy, and leisure preferences of the country-side.

In the later seventeenth century, London's impact on English society seems to be more unambiguous, more generally positive. As well as the city's continuing contribu-tion as the leading social and cultural centre of national integration, metropolitan growth began to yield significant gains for the English economy. The city's success in foreign trade made it an important source of capital formation. Related to this were significant, London-led advances in credit and commercial facilities, in insurance, transport, shipping, and industrial activity. This positive contribution

still involved heavy costs, however. The capital's exter-
minating propensities were now a major obstacle to national demographic growth at a time when the population
was stagnant and most commentators were arguing that
the country was under-populated. London's increasingly-
sophisticated, marketing operation was also causing serious
difficulties for most middling and smaller country towns.
Moreover, for all London's commercial success, the city
played only a limited role in provincial enterprise. True,
there was major metropolitan investment in land, but, so far
as we can see, Londoners did not take a leading part in
agricultural improvement. Their investment in provincial
trade and industry was generally on a small scale. Exceptions
usually owed more to accident than design. Thus the
injection of city funds into the trading economy of Liverpool
in the 1670s resulted from the flight there of city merchants
after the Great Fire. In fact, the initiative and enterprise
evident in the new industrial towns like Manchester and
Birmingham demonstrates that London's dominance was not
absolute; as the eighteenth century was to show, the provinces still had their own major role to play.

Turning from the broader impact of metropolitan growth
to the changing nature of metropolitan society itself, we can
point to developments which in many ways transformed the
shape of the urban community. The face of the city in 1700
looked very different from that of two centuries earlier. Many
of the city churches had been rebuilt by Wren in the classical
style; there were Palladian mansions and stately squares to
the west, and tightly-packed tenements to the east. The old
walled city was increasingly overshadowed by the new
suburbs, virtually cities in their own right. Fewer traders
bothered now to become freemen, the gilds decayed, and in
1712 the city abandoned its efforts to enforce the freedom on
merchants trading overseas in the joint-stock companies. The
old sense of civic community, however tenuous, was being
eroded and city government became increasingly demoralized
not least by the Crown's attack on the city's charter in the
1680s and the subsequent collapse of the Orphan's Court, a
major pillar of city finance. At the same time, like Venice and

Amsterdam before it, London was now a great cosmopolitan centre with large colonies of Jews, French Huguenots, and other aliens.

Again, however, we must be careful not to overstress the novel and unique aspects of the later Stuart capital. In 1700 the pedestrian could still walk fairly quickly across its diameter. He could also see many familiar sights like the town gates and the cramped streets of the old city. One must remember, too, that many of the new buildings were not the result of deliberate urban planning, but of the Great Fire, and even then the conservatism of the corporation and citizens meant that the opportunity was squandered. Wren's comprehensive plans for rebuilding were largely ignored and much of the ground-plan of the old city was preserved. Other changes in the metropolitan community also owed a good deal to the Fire. The decay of the gild companies and the growing insolvency of city government stemmed, at least in part, from the flight of city traders and merchants out of the old town in the wake of the conflagration. Here, at least, major changes were the product, not of an essentially 'modern' form of urban growth, but of a particular natural calamity. In other areas, important developments, like the declining sense of civic community and the enhanced social stratification, were not peculiar to London but reflected general urban developments throughout the country.

Despite all the repercussions of its expansion, the city still retained important traditional features and attitudes. While large profits were to be made in speculative colonial commerce, most city merchants exhibited a more cautious business approach relying on the older, established trades. While there were new, larger-scale industries around the port, most industrial activity was still organized in small-scale units—a feature of London's economy until well into the nineteenth century. While London was now the largest urban community in western Europe, its inhabitants still showed a penchant for less rational, more traditional, ideas and beliefs. On May Day, for instance, the chimney-sweeps —their faces whitened and their heads framed in periwigs— banged their brushes and scrapers in a noisy masquerade which has analogies with the ritualized reversal of roles found in rural folk customs. No less rustic and traditional is the story told by John Aubrey in the 1690s, that on Midsummer Eve young women went searching in metropolitan fields 'for coal under the root of a plantain, to put under their heads that night and they should dream who would be their husbands'. Such conservatism was hardly surprising. For all its size and relative importance, London was part and parcel of a society where nearly 80 per cent of the population still lived outside towns.

6

The Demographic Background

In the preceding discussion of the different categories of English town we have seen the importance of changes in the size of urban populations. Not only did such changes reflect the vacillating economic fortunes of an urban centre; they also acted as independent variables decisively affecting the quality of life in towns. Demographic developments, therefore, merit prior consideration in any account of the more important general features of urban society. In the centuries between 1500 and 1700 most English towns witnessed long periods of demographic growth, but they also suffered from frequent, and often severe, short-term demographic crises. Each of these circumstances imposed separate stresses on the social fabric of towns. The paradoxical coincidence of years of high mortality with a long-term increase in numbers was made possible only by a third factor, which will be a recurring topic throughout this chapter. This was rapid and substantial migration from countryside to town, which involved additional pressures to which local economic and social structures had to adapt.

Any precise analysis of these quantitative changes in urban demography is impossible because of the absence of reliable contemporary statistics. The work of the first political arithmeticians casts a flickering light on some parts of our subject at the end of the seventeenth century. But for earlier periods the historian must rely on parish registers, censuses of communicants, taxation assessments, and bills of mortality; all of them compiled for different purposes and all subject to distortion by a degree of geographical mobility of population which still requires investigation. Nevertheless, patient local research has begun to illuminate pieces of the demographic jigsaw and to bring its general features, if not its precise components, into sharper focus.

Table 1

The Population of some English Towns

	c.1520	c.1603	c.1670	c.1695
London (metropolitan)	60,000	200,000	—	575,000
Norwich	12,000	15,000	—	29,332
Bristol	10,000	12,000	—	19,403
York	8,000	11,000	12,000	—
Exeter	8,000	9,000	12,500	—
Salisbury	8,000	7,000	—	6,976
Coventry	6,601	6,500	—	6,710
Bury St. Edmunds	3,550	4,500	6,200	—
Leicester	3,000	3,500	5,000	—
Warwick	2,000	3,000	3,300	—
Ashby de la Zouch	?800	1,200	1,130	—
Hitchin	?650	1,800	2,400	—
East Dereham	600	1,100	1,500	—

Between 1500 and 1700 the population of England roughly doubled. The proportion of the population living in towns rose considerably faster, possibly twice as fast: in this sense it was a period of urbanization. As the figures for a sample of towns collected in Table 1 make clear, however, growth in the urban sector was unevenly distributed. Although few towns entirely stagnated, some expanded more rapidly than others. At least half the urban increase was due to the extraordinary growth of London, which by the end of our period contained 10 per cent of the country's population. Some of it was due, as we saw earlier, to the rising populations of the newer industrial and dockyard towns in the middle and later seventeenth century. In the later sixteenth century, however, the most conspicuous examples of population increase were probably provided by the smaller market-towns like Hitchin and Ashby de la Zouch, profiting from the expansion of internal trade in the decades after 1570. This same expansion gave even tinier places, like Hallaton and Billesdon in Leicestershire, a temporary prosperity as growing market centres with some rudimentary urban functions. The larger established towns of medieval England had a more uneven development. Some of them, like Bristol and Norwich, after periods of stagnation in the sixteenth century, were centres of growth in the seventeenth. Others, like Coventry, Winchester, and Salisbury, had populations little different or even smaller in 1700 than they had been in 1500. Yet even these towns had often experienced some demographic growth in the interim, periods of falling population being separated by rising numbers between about 1570 and 1620.

There were thus important chronological fluctuations in the pattern of population change in towns, some of which are masked by the figures in our table. It is probable that for many, perhaps even the majority of towns, the middle decades of the sixteenth century were a period of stagnation and population decline, the result in part of successive demographic crises. Coventry provides the most extreme example: there plague and subsistence crisis caused the population to drop by a fifth between 1520 and 1523 leaving one-quarter of the city's houses empty. But in other towns, in Bristol, York, and Norwich, there were also complaints of empty houses and high death-rates, and few signs of demographic growth in the generation before the great influenza epidemic of 1558–9. Increasing populations were most general in the half-century after 1570 in spite of continuing outbreaks of plague. In many towns, however, expansion had ended by the mid-seventeenth century, when fresh epidemics and the devastation caused by the Civil War were succeeded by a period of high mortality rates. The fall in fertility and rise in mortality which evidently occurred in the small Devonshire market-town of Colyton after a major epidemic in 1645 may have been more dramatic than elsewhere; but in places such as Barnstaple, Lichfield, and Ashby de la Zouch, the middle decades of the seventeenth century witnessed significant losses of population without any early or rapid recovery. After 1660 demographic growth appears to have been confined largely to the greatest urban centres (often ports), and the new dockyard and industrial towns. Though the precise timing and location of these variations are still obscure, it is clear that the growth of urban populations was not continuous. Nonetheless, few towns were unaffected by the general trend at some point between 1500 and 1700.

If the timing of population growth varied from town to town, so did its causes. In some places and some periods, growth could take place partly through the natural increase of an urban population. Historians have rightly stressed the high death-rates common in the unhealthy conditions of pre-industrial English towns. Infant mortality was particularly high, often more than 200 per thousand live births. The figure was 235 per thousand in one of the richer York parishes, St. Michael le Belfry, in the 1570s, and 256 in one of the poorest parishes in London, St. Botolph without Bishopsgate, in the first three years of the seventeenth century. But it was lower in the less populous market-towns, apparently as low as 150, for example, in Tudor Colyton, and hence less of a check to population increase. And even in the largest towns mortality rates varied over time and were often worse in the later seventeenth century than they had been earlier. In St. Botolph's Bishopsgate, London, the death-rate has been estimated at 29 per thousand in 1600 (slightly lower in fact than the birth-rate); by the 1690s, however, it was as high as 45 per thousand in some of the London suburbs and reached 37 per thousand even in the richer parishes in the heart of the city.

Hence it would be a mistake to exaggerate the role of towns as 'consumers of men' throughout our period. Even in the most crowded urban communities there was sometimes some slight capacity for natural growth, and outside the largest cities the picture was more favourable still. Comparison of the number of burials and baptisms in smaller towns often suggests a surprisingly healthy balance between births and deaths, and hence urban populations which were more than reproducing themselves. In Barnstaple, for instance, during the century after 1540 baptisms exceeded burials by 2,500 at a time when the population was growing from about 2,000 to roughly 4,000. The growth of towns like Stafford and

Gloucester in the same period can similarly be explained by a surplus of births over deaths, if one assumes that there was little migration out of the town. In the larger town of Exeter, in spite of successive epidemics of plague, the overall picture was as healthy: there were 5,000 more baptisms than burials between 1571 and 1700 while the population grew by approximately the same number; only after 1700 did burials exceed baptisms.

Nevertheless, in other towns (usually the larger centres) the balance of births and deaths was undoubtedly adverse for much of the period between 1540 and 1700. In Plymouth, for example, there were rather more burials than baptisms between 1582 and 1640, when the population nevertheless doubled. Likewise, there were deficits in towns like Crediton and Maldon, although in the second case the population total remained the same and in the former it rose rapidly. In Norwich, where the mayor's court gathered weekly statistics, there were nearly 10,000 more deaths than births between 1582 and 1646; yet the population, far from declining, rose by at least 5,000. Recurrent outbreaks of plague were largely responsible for this surge of mortality, and they had even more marked effects on demographic trends in London. According to statistics compiled from the bills of mortality by John Graunt, burials outnumbered baptisms between 1604 and 1643 by 100,000, and nearly three-quarters of the surplus was attributed to plague.

In some towns, therefore, only considerable and rapid migration from the countryside can account for continuing urban growth. It has been estimated that the net rate of immigration into Norwich must have been at a level of some 400 newcomers a year at the end of the seventeenth century. London's demands on the population of surrounding counties were, of course, far greater. By 1700 about 8,000 immigrants a year were needed simply to maintain its population, and, taking into account the flow of migrants out of London, the gross total was probably 50 per cent or so higher. Mobility on this scale implies that something approaching a sixth of the population of England may have had experience of life in London at the end of our period, and the attraction of the metropolis was certainly felt over considerable distances. In the Shropshire village of Myddle, for example, one in six of the families at the end of the seventeenth century had at least one member who had spent some time in the capital. If London was in a class of its own in its dependence on immigration, other towns also required steady reinforcements from the countryside. Even where mortality was low and fertility high, natural growth was often insufficient to produce the demographic increases which occurred. The population of Worcester, for instance, rose from 4,250 in 1563 to 8,000 in 1646. High fertility in the early sixteenth century and low child mortality in the early seventeenth produced a surplus of baptisms over burials which could account for half of this increase. But the rest must have been the consequence of immigration.

The vital importance of migration for the growth of urban populations can be deduced in these instances from simple sums of births and deaths. In the case of other towns, such as Exeter, Barnstaple, and Stafford, where the parish registers indicate an excess of births sufficient to explain actual increases in population, we can be less sure about the volume of immigration. But there can be no doubt that it occurred. There was a sizeable influx of Welsh migrants into Stafford in the seventeenth century; the parish register of Barnstaple indicates a high turnover of population in the sixteenth century; and the records of Exeter reveal the same acute concern with immigrant craftsmen and paupers as in other large towns. Here immigration was essential for the maintenance of urban populations because of other fundamental demographic features of early modern towns, and these must be considered before we examine the movements and motives of migrants more closely.

In the first place there were the unknown, probably large, numbers who moved out of towns and who had to be replaced. Besides successful merchants moving into landed society, they included young men and women for whom urban residence was only a temporary experience. One important influence here was the unbalanced sex ratio of many pre-industrial urban populations. Several English towns contained more adult women than men. There were eighty-seven males for every hundred females in forty London parishes in 1695, as few as eighty-three in Lichfield in the same year, and only eighty in Bristol at the same time. For the surplus women the chances of marriage depended on migration, and it is likely that there was considerable movement of young girls out of domestic service in towns, as well as into it.

Secondly, it is clear that even in relatively healthy towns the balance of births and deaths varied markedly between different sections of the population and that among the poorer classes natural population growth was unlikely. Thus in spite of the overall surplus of births over deaths in Exeter between 1571 and 1700, the poor and populous suburban parish of St. Sidwell's recorded more burials than baptisms. Here normal mortality rates were comparatively high and outbreaks of bubonic plague had their worst effects. The population of the parish, nevertheless, doubled over the whole period and it is unlikely that much of this can be accounted for by movement from other parishes in the town. The same geographical differences can be seen in other towns like Gloucester, where the number of baptisms was greater than that of burials between 1562 and 1641 in all parishes except the poorest, St. Aldate's. In fact the larger English towns did not display a single uniform demographic structure, but a range of structures reflecting socially disparate neighbourhoods. In several provincial towns as well as in London the poorer parishes had lower fertility and higher mortality rates than their more prosperous neighbours, and hence smaller proportions of children in their populations and a smaller average size of household. For such parishes immigration was a demographic necessity.

Thirdly, even towns with a favourable balance of births over deaths experienced short-term demographic crises which decimated their populations and encouraged an immediate influx of newcomers, seizing the housing and employment opportunities which epidemic disease had created. It is striking that in almost all towns populations recovered rapidly after these crises: baptisms and marriages reached their usual levels within one or two years, and many of the young adults responsible were fresh immigrants into towns. Together, mortality crises and migration did much to determine the pace and quality of demographic change in urban communities of all kinds, and we shall consider each of these features in turn.

By the sixteenth century epidemics of bubonic plague had ceased to be a familiar scourge in rural England. But they remained a recurrent cause of suffering, economic disruption, and social disorder in towns, and thereby served as a conspicuous and distinctive feature of urban society. The smallest towns could expect at least one major outbreak in the period; the larger towns often suffered several more between the great epidemic of 1479, which devastated numerous provincial centres, and the final invasion in 1665. In London, a quarter of the population died in the space of a few months in 1563 and further epidemics in 1593, 1603, 1625, and 1665 removed between a fifth and an eighth of the inhabitants. Norwich had six major epidemics between 1579 and 1665; Bristol lost a sixth of its population on three occasions between 1565 and 1603. Mortality rates commonly reached 10 per cent during epidemics of plague, but in the worst crises they jumped to more than 30 per cent, as in Norwich in 1579, in Newcastle in 1636–7, Lichfield in 1645–6, and worst of all, in Colchester in 1665–6 when nearly half the town's population was swept away. The enormous toll of death was only the most dramatic consequence of these crises. Even larger numbers, perhaps twice as many people as those whose names are entered in the burial registers, were incapacitated by sickness; plague totally disrupted the life of a town, causing unemployment and bringing its markets to a standstill. The result was often a shortage of food to add to the ravages of disease. A third of the population of Salisbury during the plague of 1627 was reported to be 'sick of the famine and many of them begin to look as green and pale as death'.

Epidemics of bubonic plague were undoubtedly the most destructive and disruptive occasions in the life of pre-industrial towns, but they were not the only causes of urban mortality crises. The influenza epidemic of 1557–9 affected all towns whose burial registers have been examined. Sieges during the Civil War brought outbreaks of typhus to Oxford, Bristol, and Plymouth. There were also crises of subsistence when harvests failed and food prices rose. The crisis in Coventry in the early 1520s is the most serious which has yet been discovered, but there may have been others elsewhere in the first decades of the sixteenth century. In Bristol in 1524 there was 'such a scarcity of corn that . . . bread was made of acorns and fern-roots', while in Norwich three years later, 'there was so great scarceness of corn that . . . the commons of the city were ready to rise upon the rich men'.

In the following century the problem of provisioning urban populations remained a critical one whenever grain prices rose. Some of the worst shortages occurred in the later 1590s, as in Barnstaple in 1596 where it was said that 'but little comes to market and such snatching and catching for that little and such a cry that the like never was heard'. Popular disorder was a common consequence inside towns and, as in epidemics of plague, tensions between town and town, and town and country, were heightened by competition for grain supplies. There were food riots in Norwich in 1532, London in 1595, and Reading in 1631; and riotous assaults on those transporting grain out of towns in Taunton in 1536, Basingstoke in 1595, Canterbury in 1596, Southampton in 1608, and Leicester in 1618. In 1586 'great numbers of weavers, tuckers and other persons most poor' assembled outside Gloucester and stopped the movement of grain up and down the Severn.

These shortages caused malnutrition and rising death-rates in many urban communities, although their effects (in so far as they can be investigated from urban parish registers after 1538) were never as severe as they had been in Coventry in the 1520s or as they were in some contemporary continental towns. The crisis of the 1590s was certainly the worst: there are occasional references to simple starvation, more common allusions to typhus, as in London, and to the effects of dysentery elsewhere. In Barnstaple, Tamworth, and several other towns, mortality rates doubled in 1597. As in epidemics of plague, however, the situation was worst in the poorest areas of the larger towns. In four suburban parishes of Bristol in 1597, for example, the death-rate climbed to three times its normal level, while it did not rise at all in the central parishes. Both plague and food shortages had their chief effects, as it was remarked in Leicester in 1626, 'in back lanes and remote places, not in the heart of the town'. They served to underline and to aggravate the social disparities between different areas of pre-industrial towns.

Mortality crises were thus the most important of the factors which made immigration a necessary ingredient in urban demography and rapidly changing populations a striking feature of urban life, especially among the poor. In some towns they produced a situation in which the majority of adults were immigrants. Evidence from ecclesiastical court cases, for example, indicates that little more than 10 per cent of the witnesses living in Canterbury and the East End of London in the later sixteenth and early seventeenth centuries were actually born there. Even in the small town of Maldon with its stagnant population, nearly half the adult men resident in the 1570s can be identified as immigrants. One London parson commented in Elizabeth's reign that every twelve years 'the most part of the parish changes, as I by experience know, some going and some coming'.

The importance of migration into towns during this period can be demonstrated without too much trouble. There are rather more difficulties when we try to explain why so many migrants took the road from the village into town. Almost certainly many factors influenced their decision. On the one hand, acting as an incentive was the general lure of the town with its prospects of employment, wealth, diversion, advancement, and charitable relief. On the other, numerous rural pressures encouraged mobility. These included the general practice of putting adolescent children out to service, and the effects of inheritance customs like primogeniture which limited the local opportunities for naturally growing populations. The problem lies in identifying the relative importance of these various pressures at different times and for different groups of migrants.

It may be suggested, however, that there were three different sorts of migration to towns. The first, which has been termed *betterment* migration, involved determined moves to a town by those aspiring to social and economic improvement. It included tradesmen and prosperous craftsmen, deliberately moving with their families in search of economic opportunities, and girls moving in the hope of gaining domestic service. But it was most clearly exemplified by the movement of adolescents to apprenticeship, and hence, through eventual freedom and minor civic and gild office, to full assimilation into the social hierarchy of a town. This sort of migration was often over short distances, relying on family connections between a town and its local hinterland and forming established links with particular villages and local economies: hence the links between the Norwich textile trades and the cloth-weaving villages of Norfolk. Apprenticeship connections might be established over greater distances too, particularly in the case of the major cities. Norwich had particular ties with the Yorkshire dales, while 9 per cent of apprentices in Bristol in the mid-sixteenth century had come from the highland zones of the North and the West. However, this long-distance element in *betterment* migration may well have declined in the course of the seventeenth century: towns were tending to take more apprentices from their own populations (perhaps because migration out of towns declined), and local opportunities presented by the growth of new towns in the North and the Midlands progressively reduced the attraction of more distant centres. The later seventeenth century saw a marked increase in the proportion of apprentices recruited locally in Northampton, Norwich, and Southampton, as well as in London. In general we may conclude that *betterment* migrants moved short distances and that their mobility was planned and deliberate.

More haphazard was the movement of poorer sections of the population, the victims of overpopulation in the country-side attracted by the promise of employment, charity, or crime in a town and liable to move long distances and from town to town when their hopes were dashed. Evidence for this kind of mobility, which has been termed *subsistence* migration, is less easily found than for more prosperous migrants. But it is clear from court depositions of migrants to Kentish towns that servants and poorer craftsmen travelled further than their social betters, while at the lowest level of the social hierarchy we have substantial evidence for the long-distance mobility of vagrants caught tramping through the streets of towns like Colchester and Salisbury. These pauper migrants, a fifth of whom had wandered more than a hundred miles, were already a pressing social problem for towns by 1518 when Coventry and London took special action against them. By the end of the century they over-shadowed all other classes of immigrants. Their numbers were especially swollen in years of bad harvest like those of the later 1590s, when the inhabitants of Carlisle, for instance, found themselves 'greatly molested with the poor that is strangers'; and the problem probably reached its peak in the early seventeenth century. Only after 1660, with the slowing down of national population growth and the enforcement of the Act of Settlement of 1662, were the pressures of pauper migration significantly alleviated.

A special group of immigrants to English towns, who shared some of the characteristics of both *betterment* and *subsistence* migrants, were alien refugees from overseas. There were, of course, sizeable communities of foreign merchants in ports like London and Southampton in the early sixteenth century and small groups of French Huguenot immigrants in London, Norwich, and other towns after 1685. But the largest influx was that of Walloon and Dutch Protestants who came from the Netherlands in the half-century after 1560. By 1568 there were more than 6,000 of them in London; and there were large communities also in towns like Sandwich, Canterbury, Southampton, Colchester, and particularly Norwich, where almost a third of the 15,000 inhabitants may have been Walloon or Dutch in the 1570s. Although they were welcomed for their introduction of new industries like the new draperies, which revived the declining economies of some towns, it is clear that most of the refugees were poor, if often skilled artisans, and they brought with them all the problems of poverty, overcrowding, and social conflict associated with later immigrant communities. There were riots against the foreigners who crowded into the industrial, northern parishes of Norwich in the later years of Elizabeth's reign, allegations that they encouraged epidemic disease, jealousy of their economic success, and fears of the potential threat implied by a fresh influx of poor labourers. Foreign refugees demonstrated in acute form the many problems which immigrants faced, and caused, on their arrival.

Taken in conjunction, rapid immigration, recurrent mortality crises, and population growth undoubtedly applied critical pressures to the social and administrative structures of early modern towns. One fundamental problem was the orderly assimilation into urban society of a heterogeneous transient population. Communities of foreigners, isolated in separate religious congregations and speaking different languages, presented obvious difficulties in this respect. But the decline of foreign immigration in the early seventeenth century led to their steady integration into English society. The constant stream of English immigrants presented more permanent problems. *Betterment* migrants could depend on the institutions of apprenticeship, civic freedom, and craft gilds as formal mechanisms easing their entry into urban society. Yet even they found difficulty in scaling the various obstacles which town oligarchies created to prevent their rise to the top in the urban hierarchy. At the same time the sheer number of apprentices in most towns made them a potential source of adolescent riot and political disorder. Other classes of urban immigrant had been prepared for some features of urban life by experience of rural crafts and industries. But the majority of these poorer migrants were never integrated into the formal structures of the town since they could not afford to purchase their freedom. They were in the town, but not of it, and segregated in particular areas they created formidable problems of social control.

The poorer parishes and suburbs of towns, in fact, provided the critical arena for the various urban demographic trends which we have discussed. There alehouses and tippling houses provided temporary accommodation for new arrivals; old houses were subdivided and new tenements thrown up.

There plague and food crises had their most devastating impact. In some towns, like Norwich and York, the area within the walls was large enough to accommodate increased populations by the conversion of existing properties. Elsewhere, suburban development continued to spread along main roads, as in Leicester and Exeter, which had more than a quarter of their populations outside the walls in the sixteenth century. Inevitably, both problems were acute in London as the built-up area expanded in all directions. As early as 1545 massive metropolitan growth provoked graphic complaints of a multitude of 'small chambers, cottages, and lodgings for sturdy beggars, harlots, idle and unthrifty persons, whereby beggary, vagabuncy [vagrancy], unthriftiness, theft, pox, pestilence, infection, diseases and infirmities do ensue and daily grow to the defacing of the beauty' of the city. The problems were proportionately serious in many provincial towns, as in Swansea where in 1603 'covetousness for great rents of such as use to take tenants or inmates into their houses' had led to 'not only sufferance of ungodly living and unlawful keeping of disordered alehouses, playing and other disorders, but also great loss unto the burgesses that are bound to keep victuals and lodging and good rule.'

Town corporations strove conscientiously, but with limited success, to deal with these major problems. They tried to regulate markets in the interests of poor consumers and, until grain supplies improved at the end of the seventeenth century, they regularly purchased foreign corn for distribution to the destitute when prices rose. The rulers of Nottingham, Coventry, Yarmouth, Leicester, Bristol, and Norwich were all importing corn from Danzig in 1597 or other dearth years for sale to 'such as are not of ability to buy their corn in the market'; while London had an ambitious, if in practice inadequate, system of granaries maintained by the livery companies for just such an emergency. Against plague, town governments developed a corpus of public health regulations imposing quarantine and restricting public assemblies; yet these measures, implemented in all towns by the time of the great epidemics of 1603, were largely ignored in the severest crises. Town councils also issued a succession of by-laws aimed at improving hygiene in the streets, again with little effect. While the central thoroughfares of a town might occasionally be kept paved and relatively clean by rudimentary improvement schemes, most streets were little more than open sewers. Conditions near St. Thomas's church, Bristol, for example, were so bad in 1629 that 'people will hardly come to church by reason of the stench'. Efforts to control vagrancy and migration were as common and as futile in the years between the Reformation and the Civil War as the regular battles to suppress begging and alehouses. Even the imposition of fines for new buildings and new conversions in London, backed up by all the weight of royal proclamations and Star Chamber, became in the end little more than a lucrative licensing system.

Some of the demographic pressures which had thus strained the resources of urban corporations were reduced in the later seventeenth century. The threat of widespread malnutrition among the poor receded with improvements in English agriculture, and plague did not return after the 1660s. The problems caused by migration into towns may also have become less acute: the number of long-distance migrants into some of the Kent towns in the late seventeenth century had probably fallen by a third compared with the period 1580–1640. Admittedly, high mortality rates continued in the poorest areas of towns and may even have grown worse with the mounting incidence of smallpox, while the largest centres and the new towns continued to face the problems of unregulated growth. Nevertheless, for most towns the late seventeenth century was a period of relative demographic stability after the stresses to which they had been subjected in the century before 1660.

7

The Economy

THE sixteenth and seventeenth centuries saw marked, sometimes violent, fluctuations in the level of economic activity of
most English towns. Unfortunately, the limitations of the
surviving evidence make it impossible to quantify these
changes precisely. Apprenticeship and testamentary records,
for example, shed light only on selected areas of the urban
economy and may distort the overall picture. The use of
demographic changes as an index of economic growth is also
hazardous, involving as it does the assumption that population growth is an infallible indicator of economic expansion.
The problem particularly affects the period from 1500 to
1640, when there was often a sharp divergence between the
demographic and economic fortunes of towns. Nor are our
sources the only cause of difficulty in any analysis of the urban
economy. Broader trends are often obscured both by the
divergent behaviour of the various tiers in the urban hierarchy
and by variations in the fortunes of individual towns. Thus in
chapter two we saw how the considerable buoyancy of most
market-towns in the later sixteenth century contrasted with
the more fragile prosperity of the larger county towns.
Moreover, even within the same broad category of urban
communities there were marked variations in economic
experience. Elizabethan Worcester, for example, apparently
flourished, mainly owing to its thriving textile industry, at a
time when other cathedral cities like Canterbury, Gloucester,
and Salisbury were barely able to maintain economic
equilibrium.

Any discussion of the urban economy in our period must,
therefore, start by focusing on some of the local variables

which affected individual towns. One decisive determinant of local experience was frequently the changing relationship between the town and its hinterland. In the case of Worcester, cited earlier, it is arguable that the town's exceptional industrial prosperity in the later sixteenth century stemmed from the statute of 1533 banning cloth manufacture in the adjoining countryside. In the late seventeenth century Liverpool benefited tremendously from the increasing industrialization of the Lancashire hinterland exemplified by the rise of Manchester. Less obvious but also important were changes in the relationship of a town with other urban centres in the region. For example, the growth of Maidstone as an active marketing and service centre in mid-Kent created serious, if short-term, economic problems for its middle-rank rival, the ancient city of Rochester, only ten miles further down the Medway Valley. Another relationship which could have significant repercussions for the local urban economy was that between a town and a leading local landowner. This was particularly true of market-towns and small country centres. In the sixteenth and early seventeenth centuries the patronage of the Hastings family, earls of Huntingdon, played a major part in the economic success of Ashby. As well as securing several additional fairs for the town, the family employed local men in the household, bought from the town markets and attracted tenants and other suitors who entertained themselves in the Ashby alehouses. With the destruction of their castle at Ashby during the Civil War, the family left the town for good, almost certainly accelerating its general decay. At Sittingbourne in the late sixteenth century the hostility of William Cromer, a county magnate owning part of the market tolls of nearby Milton, prevented the town exploiting the upswing in North Kent's trade with the capital.

Other local fluctuations in urban economic activity might arise from natural calamities. As we saw in the preceding chapter, epidemics of bubonic plague were a recurrent threat in all towns for much of the period, and they inflicted serious damage on the urban economy. Those who could afford to do so fled from the disease, and rural areas and neighbouring towns tried to break off all contact with centres of infection, leaving the poorer members of an afflicted community without employment and often without food supplies. Local and long-distance trade was brought to a halt and urban administration and urban finances were left in disorder. In Manchester, for example, in 1645 'most of the inhabitants living upon trade' were 'not only ruined in their estates but many families are like to perish for want who cannot sufficiently be relieved'; a company of soldiers had to suppress the 'dangerous combinations' which resulted. In most cases urban economies recovered surprisingly quickly after these disasters. At Colchester, for example, the evidence indicates that the epidemics of 1579, 1603, 1626, 1631, 1644, and 1665–6 failed to do permanent economic damage; even after the last and worst of these, cloth production rapidly regained its normal level. But such mortality crises must certainly have impeded smooth economic growth in the larger towns, and the effects may have been more lasting in a few smaller communities. John Aubrey thought that plague was responsible for the decline of the Wiltshire market-town of Highworth, having been 'very prejudicial to the market there; by reason whereof all the country sent their cattle to Swindon market'.

Fire was another natural hazard which menaced the town economy. While the Great Fire of London is deservedly famous for its scale and cost, destroying 13,200 houses plus almost all the main city buildings, worth *in toto* about ten million pounds, nearly every English town suffered at least one major fire between 1500 and 1700. *A Lamentable Discourse on the Spoyle of East Dearham*, published in 1581, describes how a fire swept through more than fifty houses and 350 outhouses there:

> 'Some came with carts, and with whole loads of care
> Some goods did lead into the fields and way,
> Some for their deeds and evidences pray,
> Some that were stored of victuals and of grain,
> Did see it burn to their loss and pain.'

During the fire looting occurred and the total damage was estimated at £14,000—not a negligible sum for a small country town to lose. A second fire in Dereham in 1679 destroyed 170 houses and caused losses of around £19,000. Fires elsewhere were no less costly. The conflagration at Bury in 1608 devastated 160 dwelling houses and 400 outhouses: the total damage was put at £60,000. The deleterious impact on economic activity, however, far exceeded the material loss. In the case of London, the economic paralysis caused by the Great Fire prompted many merchants and traders to migrate out of the walled city into the suburbs and even as far as Ipswich, Oxford, and Liverpool. For most provincial towns the high cost of rebuilding and replacing trade stocks quickly—in order to prevent business drifting away to an urban rival—must have imposed serious strains on the urban economy. Yet, in the majority of cases, the setback was temporary. Indeed in some centres, such as Northampton and Warwick, the townsmen actually made a virtue of necessity and used the opportunity of the fire to rebuild parts of the town in a grander style with wide streets and brick houses, in order to attract the patronage of the gentry and professional men.

Silting, another species of natural enemy, posed a more severe challenge to various coastal towns in our period. In the sixteenth century there were complaints from Rye, Sandwich, Boston, Chester, and other ports, lamenting their loss of trade owing to the obstruction of their havens. At Chester the process of silting was already having an effect by 1500 and the corporation tried to overcome the problem by building a new haven out in the estuary. The new project was a failure, however, and was eventually demolished, encouraging the migration of Chester's trade to Liverpool. Not that the problem was always caused by nature. An additional factor in some places was the drainage of the hinterland marshes by improving gentry, which led to the alteration of currents in the haven. Rye, for instance, was badly affected by drainage and land reclamation in nearby Romney Marsh. Whatever the cause, most afflicted towns proved incapable of dealing with the problem. To some extent this stemmed from a lack of local expertise (though in some places a Dutch engineer was employed), but it also reflected a shortage of capital and, perhaps, an absence of civic will-power. A variation on the same theme was the choking up of inland waterways. Canterbury, Lincoln, and Exeter all suffered from this threat to their trade and shipping. Only Exeter, with its large and active business community, managed to preserve its outlet to the sea: the Topsham canal, begun in 1564, was completed despite the opposition of powerful, local land-owners like the Earl of Bedford and its expense was the greatest single investment by the town in our period.

In general, however, most of these local problems caused only short-term economic fluctuations. A town needed to be small or declining before such local events took on a major significance, and it usually required a coincidence of local difficulty and overall urban contraction to cause permanent damage. We must, therefore, widen our perspective at this point and examine the secular fluctuations affecting the urban economy during this period, at the same time making allowances for the differing experience of our main types of town.

At the end of the fifteenth century the urban sector of the English economy was still profiting from the preceding century or so of relative stability. Although some towns were evidently in decline, like Stamford, Lincoln, or Shrewsbury, the balance was more than made up by such prosperous communities as Southampton, Exeter, and Bideford. Cor-porate towns frequently preserved their specialist, industrial function, particularly the manufacture of textiles, while urban markets were beginning to exploit the slow recovery of the agrarian economy which stemmed from the revival of population growth evident by 1500. The first half of the sixteenth century was, however, a period of considerable difficulty for most town economies. As we saw in chapter two, protests poured into London from almost all the county towns of the kingdom; and leading provincial cities like Bristol, Norwich, and York were also hard hit. In the case of Bristol the anguished cries of the city fathers and the sharp decline in trade visible in the customs accounts—neither in themselves wholly conclusive pieces of evidence—are amply confirmed by the business records of John Smythe, a leading merchant of the town. From them we can see that by the 1540s Bristol and its merchants were far less wealthy than they had been a century earlier. The only obvious exception to this picture of general decline was London, which was now busily exploiting its powerful position in foreign trade and as the seat of an expanding royal government. While the numerous market-towns may also have been starting to grow, this was as yet from a low economic base.

The explanation for these difficult, if not critical, economic conditions in towns is complex and the circumstances have yet to be fully explored. At root may have been a significant switch in investment away from the towns to the countryside, both to farming and to rural industry, particularly rural cloth manufacture. This was already starting to occur before 1500, but it now gained momentum from the continuing upward trend in the agrarian economy and falling rural wage-rates. However, our knowledge of this area is still incomplete and we should not ignore other possible determinants. One may have been recurrent difficulties in foreign trade, especially in the 1520s and the 1550s, coinciding with bad harvests and high prices. Another was the high level of government taxation, again in the 1520s and in the 1540s. Finally, the Dissolution of the Monasteries dealt a serious blow to those corporate centres like Reading, St. Albans, and Canterbury which had previously benefited from the inflow of rents to urban monasteries or from the entertainment of visiting pilgrims.

In the later sixteenth century there was some improvement in the economic situation of most English towns. As we noted earlier, the older centres, whose industrial role was being eroded by rural competition, began to put increasing stress on marketing and social services: one can observe this development at Canterbury, York, Salisbury, Lincoln, and Norwich. In the latter, J. F. Pound has detected a steady rise in the number of freemen employed in clothing and distributive occupations; the number of grocers alone rose from twenty-seven in 1525 to 150 in 1569, while there was also an increase in the size of the professional trades. The middling towns were now following hard in the footsteps of London and the market-towns in exploiting the overall expansion of internal trade which was such a marked feature of Elizabethan England. Behind this expansion was a fundamental redistribution of provincial income and wealth, as population pressure gave a substantial advantage to food producers over food consumers, to the farmers and landlords over labourers and the poor. Internal trade was also undoubtedly encouraged by the political stability enforced by the later Tudor regime.

While the late sixteenth century was a period of prosperity, or at least of limited recovery, for the mass of English towns the basic weaknesses of many of the middling-sized centres remained, however, and became more obvious in the following decades. As London continued to consolidate its lead in overseas and domestic trade, many provincial towns were forced to recognize the evident disadvantages of their position, and they seized on the obvious scapegoat. The Free Trade controversy of James I's reign served not only to articulate the anger of many provincial ports at the capital's pretensions to commercial monopoly, but also acted as an outlet for the many other economic grievances of individual towns. But it was during the crises of the 1620s and 1640s that their fragile economies suffered most strain. Evidence of this is to be found for numerous established centres, from ports like Dover and Boston to such county towns as Gloucester, Dorchester, and Salisbury. In 1626 'the causes of this decay' in Gloucester were said to be 'the great fall of trade generally in this city by reason of the late great and yet continuing plague, [and] the excessive number of poor, chiefly occasioned by the decay of clothing wherein this city and county have much suffered more than other parts, here being now not above two or three clothiers and those men of mean ability, whereas we have heretofore had near twenty men of good estates who have kept great numbers of poor on work.' Here and elsewhere, from the 1620s to the 1640s, urban industry was sorely affected not only by a contraction in domestic demand, mainly caused by high food prices, but by instability in North European markets owing to the Thirty Years War. Finally, the English Civil War itself had repercussions for the urban economy, bringing widespread disruption of communications and transport, high taxation, and physical damage to several towns. At Penzance, for instance, it was said in 1648 that the town was so 'exquisitely plundered . . . as they are all utterly undone'.

In the later seventeenth century, as we saw in chapter two, there was some revival in the fortunes of a few of the larger county towns: those like Northampton and Nottingham able to enforce their predominance over lesser rivals as the single undisputed county centre. But this recovery was often at the expense of small county towns which faced a deteriorating economic position. Also in economic difficulty now were many market-towns such as Milton Regis, Ashby, Burford, and Thetford, and some at least were close to losing their urban status for good. At the other extreme, however, the improved fortunes of the more important county towns were shared, as earlier chapters have suggested, by the provincial capitals, some of the ports, the new towns, and, above all, the metropolis. In general we can discern in the later Stuart period a progressive polarization in economic fortunes within the urban hierarchy.

The origins of this polarization are probably to be found in national demographic changes: the stagnation in the country's population after the 1640s meant a recession in agricultural demand, grain prices, and farming prosperity. Though major landowners reorganized and improved their estates to counter the reduction in demand, other sectors of rural society, particularly the small landowners and tenant farmers, fared much worse. The rationalization of agricultural production and the growing concentration of landed wealth in the hands of county landowners (helped by legal developments which made it easier to entail estates and by new, securer forms of mortgage) tended to channel much of a now relatively static volume of conspicuous consumption and internal trade towards the larger provincial centres. The process was given further impetus by the steady improvement in internal communications. Turnpikes made their first real advance from the 1690s, while between 1662 and 1670 there were at least nine river navigation acts with eight more between 1697 and 1700. Compounding the decline of the smaller market centres was the growing trend away from the old style of open market with all the inconvenience of inclement weather and clumsy market regulations. Instead traders operated increasingly through the private market of the inn and public house. The latter were more congenial for business and could be found in the village as well as the market-town.

Not that the changing pattern of internal trade was the only variable in the reorganization of urban economic life during the late seventeenth century. The spa towns and the provincial capitals exploited the new tastes and fashions proclaimed by the London social élite. The larger provincial ports like Bristol, Hull, and Liverpool benefited both from the expansion of overseas trade with the colonies and Europe, and from the transformation of their hinterlands with the rise of the new industrial towns considered earlier. Industrial specialization for carefully defined markets also gave two older towns, Colchester and Norwich, economic vitality in the later seventeenth century. A further factor may also be noted here, one which involved significant changes in the nature of the town economy. As we shall see shortly, these decades witnessed a new stability, at least in the economies of the larger towns.

Our account of the main medium-term fluctuations in the fortunes of towns between 1500 and 1700 has shown the importance of five variables, all of them influencing towns from outside. These were the general population trend, the related state of the rural economy, the pattern of internal trade, the developments in international commerce, and the level of political order. No less important, however, was the basic internal structure of the town economy, and we shall briefly examine this last variable in the remainder of the chapter. For there can be little doubt that for much of the period the urban economy was characterized by a fundamental fragility. It was this long-term instability which made towns so vulnerable to the short- and medium-term pressures which we described earlier.

An important source of weakness was the high, perhaps

excessive, density of urban settlements in large parts of the country, particularly in the South and West. As we have seen, the absolute peak in the number of urban communities had been reached in the early fourteenth century and there-after there had been some decline. Consequently, the urban hierarchy was tolerably stable, but only as long as its con-stituent towns kept to their defined roles: the larger towns as industrial and longer-distance marketing centres, the smaller communities as simple marketing points servicing the local subsistence economy. The system probably worked reasonably well in the fifteenth century, but it came under increasing pressure after 1500 as the larger towns proved unable to retain their industrial function and had to empha-size their marketing and service roles. This brought them into long-term conflict with the market-towns. The expansion of inland trade in the later sixteenth century provided some room for economic manoeuvre for most types of town, but when this slowed down after the 1620s major problems arose, especially for the smaller centres.

Also critical to the structure of urban economies, mainly in the sixteenth century, was the low level of general capitali-zation and the concentration of wealth in the hands of a narrow élite. In the small Suffolk textile and market-town of Lavenham, for instance, the Spring family owned 37 per cent of the total, taxable wealth of the community at the time of the subsidy of 1524. In Coventry, at the same time, three men paid a quarter of the subsidy assessment on the town; William Wyggeston the younger alone paid a quarter of the tax assessed on Leicester. These may have been exceptional cases, but the subsidy return for Canterbury indicates a rather similar concentration of wealth: out of a working population of about 1,000 citizens only twenty-nine were assessed at more than £40. In consequence, the main economic initiative within a town often depended on a few merchant families. This in itself was hardly the best recipe for economic stability for, as we shall see in the next chapter, there was a high turnover of personnel among urban élites in the early modern period.

One might argue that the concentration of wealth did at

least lead to more effective investment of capital, encouraging for example larger units of production. But it is difficult to show that this occurred. Recent research has suggested that, even in London, the great merchants 'always distributed their capital widely, both to secure themselves against misfortunes in trade and to maximize their profits'. Although the subject has yet to be fully explored, the investment patterns of provincial merchants were probably not dissimilar. Detailed analysis of the personal wealth of Canterbury citizens before 1640 indicates that the greater merchants preferred to employ their fortunes in a wide range of investments, most of them non-productive in the strict sense. Leases, often of rural land, farmstock, and expensive household furnishings some-times comprised more than a third of a leading merchant's personal wealth; debts, frequently small, and in the case of provincial merchants often irrecoverable, might form another third; this left no more than 30–35 per cent for trade-stock, plate, and cash (the latter often forming only 5 per cent of the total). This distribution of assets was hardly surprising. As in London, leading merchants were usually conservative men, concerned to preserve their fortunes by diversifying their wealth as much as possible. At the same time their behaviour was not determined simply by economic criteria. In most cases they were also influenced by a desire to enhance their social standing; hence their substantial investment in rural property.

The basic instability of town economies probably increased during the sixteenth century. In many corporate centres the number of active urban magnates may have fallen, at least some of them discouraged by the growing burdens of civic office-holding and attracted into the countryside by the considerable profits of rural landownership. At the other end of the economic spectrum there was certainly a growth of poverty, exacerbated by the influx of rural poor. The latter aggravated urban unemployment and required a growing amount of poor relief which was mainly spent on food imported from the countryside. High poor-rates, particularly from the 1590s, may well have been a serious burden for small artisans and traders and probably depressed domestic urban demand for goods and services. All this accentuated the close economic dependence of provincial towns on the countryside. Even established towns offered little or no resistance to the vagaries of the rural economy. Serious harvest failure had immediate repercussions for the whole economic structure of a town. We can see this from the accounts of Thomas Minshull, a prosperous Nantwich mercer. In 1597 he noted that 'the gains of my shop this year by reason I bought so little wares and the great dearth' were £100, £60 less than usual; moreover, 'all the gain of my shop was spent but £5, by reason of the dearth and great charges I lived at and giving away to the poor, for corn was at such a very fearful price'.

Given this fundamental instability and vulnerability to outside pressures, it is hardly surprising that towns responded to their problems in a protectionist fashion. In the sixteenth century, craft gilds became the principal weapons of economic restriction and regulation, aimed both at reducing economic conflict within towns and at keeping outside competitors at bay. A few corporations like that at York may have been flexible enough to arrest their decay by liberalizing their trading apparatus, but this was exceptional. By 1600 elaborate and restrictive controls were in operation in most middling and larger towns, like Abingdon, Canterbury, Coventry, Gloucester, Lincoln, and Rye. Other defensive steps included prohibitions on outside traders dealing in town markets and non-freemen taking up employment. At Leicester, for instance, the tailors' gild led the attack on those 'who like drone bees to the hive, paying neither scot nor lot [i.e. town taxes], lie lurking in the suburbs and other secret places in and about this town, and rob your suppliants of the work which they should do to their great disgrace and utter undoing.' There was also a related attempt to prevent poor outsiders becoming freemen by raising the fines: thus at Rochester they more than doubled during Elizabeth's reign.

S. Kramer has argued that gild and other civic restrictions severely aggravated the economic plight of many towns in our period. The evidence for this is inconclusive, since it is always difficult to judge whether such restrictions were a cause as well as a symptom of economic distress. It is certain, however, that the elaborate machinery of protectionism failed to reverse the downward economic trend in numerous established centres. By the mid-seventeenth century, craft gilds were themselves often falling into decay. At Tewkesbury the cordwainers' company became little more than a social club; at St. Albans the number of gilds fell from four to two; at Gloucester in 1665 the butchers' gild was 'in great disorder'; at Carlisle the crafts collapsed through internal conflict; and even the London craft companies were patently losing their power by 1700. To some extent their decay may have reflected the decline of the trades they had sought to protect. But it also indicates the discrediting of the kind of commercial protectionism which they had exemplified. Whether out of choice or necessity civic policy was becoming less restrictive.

By the later seventeenth century the basic structure of town economies seemed less fragile, at any rate in the middling and larger towns. At the bottom end of the social hierarchy, the pressures had abated. With the slowing down of immigration and natural population growth the endless ranks of the destitute turned into a more distinct and manageable group of unprivileged. With fewer poor, *per capita* poor relief may even have increased, allowing recipients to buy more than bare necessities such as food. Instead of being a major drain on the urban economy, poor relief may sometimes have provided a mild stimulus to urban demand for goods and services.

The urban economy also benefited from the expansion of the economic élite. Together with the old, limited core of merchants and traders, there was now often an important group of minor gentry, who retired to the towns as rentiers in face of the growing monopoly of landownership by county magnates, as well as numerous professional men—physicians, attorneys and schoolteachers—all providing services for town and countryside. Professor Everitt's description of this new élite as a 'pseudo-gentry' is valuable in pointing out their pretensions to gentle status and life-style: but it glosses over their real importance for the town economy. Their presence was influential in a number of ways: first, it stimulated the urban land market and house-building; secondly, it encouraged internal demand for urban products and services; thirdly, it provided an important new source of local capital, for loans and credit. In this connection it may be significant that the late seventeenth century saw a distinct improvement in credit facilities in general, which helped many smaller tradesmen and craftsmen, the middling sort of townsfolk whose business-lives had always been precarious hitherto. The economic structure of towns was becoming more secure.

A final reason for the growing viability of urban economies towards the end of our period may have been the declining density of urban centres and the emergence of a new economic balance between the towns which remained. As we saw earlier, the late-seventeenth-century rationalization in marketing pushed many smaller market centres out of business, leaving the main bulk of internal trade to be handled by larger country towns and provincial capitals. The new towns confirmed rather than obscured this development: most of them had distinct specialist functions with only a limited interest in general marketing, and in the case of the industrial towns the majority were located in the North, outside the old areas of dense urban settlement. There was specialization too in the more prosperous of the older English cities, in coal at Newcastle, stuffs at Norwich, bays at Colchester, serges at Exeter. There seems by 1700 to have been a more harmonious and positive relationship between the different sorts of town. After a period of intense competition, the successful survivors had begun to develop economic functions which complemented rather than rivalled one another.

The period from 1500 to 1700 was a time of serious and often prolonged economic difficulty for many English towns, only excepting London. The impact both of short-term, local pressures and of more general, medium-term trends was greatly aggravated by the structural weaknesses both within the urban hierarchy and inside the economies of most towns. By 1700, however, towns had often acquired a new economic stability and resilience which would allow them to survive future crises with greater equanimity.

8

The Social Structure

THE social structure of English towns in the sixteenth and seventeenth centuries can be analysed in two ways: first, through a static description of its shape and component parts; and secondly, through a discussion of the extent of mobility both within the structure and into it from outside. For urban society in this period presents a picture both of a clear and relatively rigid social pyramid of wealth and status and of a social hierarchy whose individual members were constantly changing. This was because status and power in towns were clearly related to levels of wealth. They were less confused than in the countryside by values placed on ownership of land or the social prestige implied by a family's name or style of life. Moreover, in urban society wealth might be fairly quickly won—though more so at some periods than others—and even more quickly lost. Whereas those who rose to wealth through urban employments have had their achievements chronicled in the histories of many towns, those who failed to make their fortunes and sank back into obscurity were undoubtedly much more common. There must have been many like the Lancaster tradesman who, in the 1680s by 'neglect of his business and expensive living', had 'over run his credit and was forced to give over his trade'. Wealth and the status it brought with it could be fragile acquisitions in urban society.

Nevertheless, they made an indelible mark upon the social structure. When we analyse, on the basis of taxation returns, the pyramid of wealth in early modern English towns, we discover the base to be very broad, rising to a sharp, narrow peak. The sources most commonly used for this purpose at the beginning of our period are the thorough subsidy assessments of 1523–5. These reveal a common pattern of wide extremes of wealth and poverty. At the bottom were those exempted from the subsidy altogether because they had neither wages nor goods worth £1 a year: the unemployed, or under-employed, and the destitute. Such people amounted to almost half the population of the impoverished town of Coventry, and a third or slightly more of the inhabitants of Exeter, Worcester, and Leicester. Those tax-payers assessed only on wages cannot have been much more fortunate: the wage-earning class amounted to well over a third of the taxable population of the largest towns, 43 per cent in Leicester, 47 per cent in Exeter, 48 per cent in Salisbury. Taking these two groups together, we can conclude that as much as two-thirds of the urban population in the 1520s lived below or very close to the poverty line. Above them were the independent craftsmen, employers, and merchants who made up that third of the population which enjoyed relative property and comfort. Even here a steep pyramid structure is evident. At its peak were those assessed at more, often much more, than £40 in property and they formed between 4 and 6 per cent of the taxable population of towns like Norwich, Exeter, and Leicester. Thus a few tycoons monopolized large fractions of personal wealth in many urban communities. In both Exeter and Coventry, 7 per cent of the taxable population owned almost two-thirds of the taxable wealth of the town.

Variations, of course, occurred between towns. The largest communities, especially those which combined the functions of industrial centres and ports, had the largest groups of tycoons and poor. In smaller centres and market-towns, wealth was more equally distributed. Aylesbury, for example, had only a little over 1 per cent of its taxable population assessed on more than £40, and only 26 per cent assessed on wages and goods worth £1, compared with 5 per cent and 40 per cent in the same categories in Norwich. Worcester, without a large mercantile élite but with its dependence on the cloth industry, had 2 per cent and 44 per cent of its taxable population in these groups. If the proportion in the various economic groups differed from town to town, so did the wealth of the more prosperous inhabitants. The average estate bequeathed by London merchants in the sixteenth and early seventeenth centuries was more than five times as great as that of provincial merchants, while mercantile fortunes in Bristol and Exeter were often three times greater than the largest to be found in Leicester. But in all towns the obvious gulf was that between rich and poor. While Worcester clothiers left fortunes fifty times the size of those of most labourers, the wealth of London merchants was at least a hundred times greater than that of metropolitan artisans, and there were enormous numbers of people below them with no property at all.

It is impossible to assess with any accuracy the ways in which the distribution of wealth in urban society changed between 1500 and 1700. The Hearth Tax returns of the 1660s and 1670s, which have often been used for analysis of the social structure, are not directly comparable with the subsidies of the 1520s; neither can they tell us anything about the important changes which may have occurred during the last decades of our period. They suggest, however, that the rough shape of the social pyramid in towns had altered relatively little since the early sixteenth century. At the top we still have a comfortable group, roughly a quarter of urban populations, living in houses with more than two hearths, and within this class a wealthy élite of 1 or 2 per cent with more than nine hearths. At the other extreme, the bottom three-quarters of the population includes a broad substratum of poor householders exempted from the Hearth Tax altogether. Unfortunately, the grounds for exemption are not directly comparable with those of 1523–5 and they may well have varied from place to place. But those exempted frequently formed 40 per cent of urban householders and sometimes even more. In the large industrial towns of Colchester and Norwich the proportions reached 52 per cent and 62 per cent. In the small weaving towns of Braintree and Bocking, which had no mercantile élite, no less than 67 per cent and 81 per cent of householders were too poor to pay. The proportions were considerably and consistently smaller only in county and social capitals like York (20 per cent exempted) which had lost their older industrial function, and in stagnant market-towns such as Ashby de la Zouch (23 per cent) and Melton Mowbray (16 per cent) which were no longer attracting local immigrants.

There was, therefore, no major restructuring of the social hierarchy in English towns between the 1520s and the 1660s. It is likely, however, that there were small but significant shifts in the distribution of wealth in some urban centres and, in particular, that the gulf between rich and poor generally widened. Even allowing for the economic problems of towns during our period, urban fortunes could still be rapidly augmented in particular towns, as from foreign trade in London or from the cloth industry of later Stuart Exeter. The richest Exeter merchants were amassing considerable wealth in the course of the seventeenth century and by its end their incomes were often comparable to those of county landowners. At the same time, increases in population, immigration of paupers, and the fact that wages lagged behind escalating prices for most of our period, meant that the numbers of poor rose sharply and their condition grew steadily worse. The polarization between rich and poor was also made more conspicuous by social zoning within towns, the most prosperous areas being rebuilt, often in brick, for merchants and gentry residents, while the labouring classes were crowded into one- or two-room hovels in the suburbs. Thus, by 1600, the northern parishes of King's Lynn, the southern parts of Southampton, and the centres of Norwich and Bristol were residential as well as business areas for the well-to-do. There were significant complaints in Norwich in 1563 that 'gentlemen come to the city to buy up the houses and to pull down poor folks houses to the intent that they would not have poor people to dwell near unto them'.

The middling sort, those at neither extreme of the social scale, may have found little improvement in their economic condition—at least until the last decades of the period. Certainly, if we allow for inflation, the average testator in Worcester was no more wealthy in the mid-seventeenth century than he had been in the mid-sixteenth. But he may well have spent his wealth in a different way. For like his richer betters he too was improving and embellishing his house, putting glass in the windows, buying more changes of clothing, more furniture, and more books. As early as 1582 a critical observer of the more prosperous citizens of Southampton noted caustically: 'Then must every man of good calling be furnished with change of plate, with great store [of] fine linen, rich tapestry and all other things which might make show of bravery.' Respectable citizens, and even their servants, increasingly imitated the consumption patterns of the gentry, thereby confirming the growing separation between those with property and those without.

The distribution of wealth and its display are, however, only the first of the yardsticks by which one can measure the contours of a social structure. The distribution of status and power are equally significant. Neither of these invariably coincides with economic gradations, of course, but in early modern towns they almost always did so. The vital status distinction in most boroughs and corporate towns was that separating the freemen from the rest. Only freemen had political rights, as the 'commonalty' of the town, and only freemen might legally engage in independent trade. The non-free were treated as 'foreigners'. The freedom was thus the clearest indicator of formal class distinctions in early modern towns and it was gained by inheritance, apprenticeship, marriage, or purchase—the price of the latter method often increasing rapidly in the course of the period. The number of men who enjoyed the privilege varied from town to town: they formed 80 per cent of all householders in early Tudor Coventry; perhaps half the adult males in Tudor York and later Stuart Norwich; something like a quarter of the householders in Colchester at the end of the seventeenth century. The average, however, was between a half and a third of the adult male population and there can be little doubt that the freemen group was roughly equivalent to the upper ranks of the tax-paying classes in the 1523–5 subsidy.

Among the freemen there were further status distinctions, just as there were differing degrees of wealth. Membership of religious gilds and craft fellowships provided a framework of differentiation: wardens and liverymen in gilds and companies took precedence over ordinary gild members, while some mercantile gilds—usually those of the Mercers or Grocers— carried greater prestige than the artisan companies such as the tanners or glovers. Towns expressed their individuality in the number and composition of the gilds and companies which embodied and helped to define their social, political, and economic élite. The Twelve Great Livery Companies of London provide the most famous example of the prestige and power of a select few of these associations, and even many smaller towns had a quite elaborate structure of companies. But common to all such craft fellowships was the close identification between their rulers and the political and economic élite of the town. The richest men in Exeter, Norwich, and London were not only aldermen and councillors, but also leading figures in the most important of the town's gilds.

We shall discuss the political significance of this plutocracy, its role as an oligarchy, in the next chapter. For the moment it is sufficient to stress the ways in which it expressed and supported its economic position by the impressive trappings of office and authority in civic and gild institutions. In the course of our period craft companies often lost their vocational unity as the economic interests of their members diversified. Yet they remained as wealthy social clubs giving prestige to an oligarchic élite. In the same way, the freedom itself, which by the late seventeenth century had often lost much of its economic justification as non-freemen increasingly evaded civic controls, continued to retain its function as a mark of social distinction. The concern of the élite to maintain such distinctions is also evidenced by their enthusiasm in prosecuting attacks on their 'reverence', 'dignity' and 'worship' in the courts, and by their endeavours to regulate the dress and precedence of the various degrees of citizens. On Sundays, feast days, and other official occasions, mayors and aldermen (and often their wives) paraded in scarlet gowns and the junior councillors followed them in more sober black. Not only grand ceremonial processions, but the order of seating at church, were subjects of serious magisterial concern. Thus at St. Nicholas's church, Liverpool in 1685

it was ordered that 'no person under the degree of an alderman shall sit in the aldermen's seat without licence from
Mr. Mayor and [the] chapelwardens. That none under the
degree of an alderman's wife shall sit in the seat next unto the
aldermen without licence', and so on, ending with the in-
junction 'that all apprentices and servants shall sit or stand
in the alleys according to ancient custom'. Thus, although
the social structure of English towns was determined essentially by wealth, it is evident that in the larger centres it was
embellished by an array of institutions and regulations which
conveyed and defined power and status.

So far we have examined the social structure of English
towns in essentially static terms. But it is important to ask
how rigid these economic and status distinctions were, to
investigate how much mobility there was across social
boundaries. It is clear to begin with that the urban élite was
constantly changing. There was a variety of reasons for this.
High mortality rates brought some mercantile families to an
end, at least in the male line, leaving daughters and widows
to provide opportunities for social mobility through marriage
or remarriage. In some towns a third of the office-holders
died without surviving sons, while the estates of at least a fifth
of the mayors of Exeter between 1564 and 1613 came into the
town's orphan's court because no heir was of age. Secondly,
business fortunes were fragile and commercial wealth often
transient. Dependence on primitive and unreliable forms of
credit, interruptions in the flow of trade because of war
abroad or dearth and plague at home, extravagance, or bad
luck, all put pressure on business fortunes. The risks were
most alarming where the rewards were greatest, in government finance or international trade. Thus, it is not surprising
to find that only 37 per cent of a sample of London aldermen
between 1586 and 1612 had children who achieved the wealth
or status of their fathers. For these reasons the urban
nouveaux riches were tempted to diversify in an attempt to find
safer forms of investment. For the first three-quarters of our
period this frequently led to a movement in investment away
from the urban sector into land. In Elizabeth's reign alone,
half a dozen of the richest merchants of Exeter founded

landed families, while most London aldermen and councillors had landed property, and many looked to this to protect their children from the risks and cares of commercial life.

It is important not to exaggerate this movement from urban society into the landed classes. It was the mark only of the minority, of the especially successful, and it was the climax to a rapid accumulation of wealth which usually only occurred in the cloth industry before 1550 or in international trade in the major ports during the later sixteenth and seventeenth centuries. In the case of lesser towns like Northampton and Ipswich, movement out of the élite was less rapid and there the same families might be prominent throughout our period, as the Daundys and Bloyses were at Ipswich. Unhappily, we know less about these smaller towns than about those where success was quicker and movement more tempting. It is also probable that even in the larger towns this sort of mobility declined in the later seventeenth century. The growing stock market, the Bank of England and more stable government finance, the expanding professions, and the purchase of urban property all now provided secure investment for commercial capital in competition with rural estates. Here were the beginnings of a permanent financial 'interest' and of a class with the tastes, wealth, and leisure of the gentry, but an urban residence. Nevertheless, until the later seventeenth century, the indications are that there was a rapid turnover in the economic élite of the greater urban centres. Only eleven men followed their fathers into the council of Tudor Worcester, for example, and it was still rare for successful urban families to stay in a major city for more than three generations.

Yet the fact that the composition of the élite was constantly changing does not necessarily mean that there was considerable upward social mobility in these larger towns. There were, no doubt, some 'unfree' inhabitants who managed to raise the capital to purchase their freedom, just as there were some lesser tradesmen who were able to apprentice their sons to members of more prestigious gilds, and some apprentices who married the widows of their masters. But the barriers to this sort of internal mobility were formidable ones, requiring capital and influence to overcome the exclusive prejudices of the élite. The channels of entry into the ranks of great trading institutions like the Merchant Adventurers, for example, became increasingly narrow in the course of the sixteenth century. As a result, the clearest examples of upward social mobility in the major urban centres were provided by the rise not of individuals but of whole trades or groups of trades, who replaced the older élites and often shook political and economic institutions in the process. Examples of this can be seen in the rise of butchers and tanners to predominance over the wool-merchants of Leicester at the end of the sixteenth century, or in the replacement of the Merchant Adventurers by the Levant and East India interests as the pre-eminent merchant group in London a few decades later. Unless the economic circumstances and institutional frameworks which dictated the distribution of wealth and status were radically changed in this way, it was difficult for individuals to make much headway against them.

In many towns it was probably more common for vacant places in the urban élite to be filled by relative newcomers to the community than by families which had steadily clambered up from its lower reaches. Less than 10 per cent of the greater merchants of London in the sixteenth and early seventeenth centuries are known to have been born in the capital; three-quarters of its Elizabethan mayors were first generation Londoners. This reliance on newcomers was less marked in other towns, but it was not absent. Half of the ruling élite of Tudor Worcester, for example, were recent immigrants to the town. These new recruits had often come from relatively prosperous sections of the rural community or from families which had already begun to rise in other smaller towns. By the middle of the seventeenth century nearly half the freemen of the Drapers' Company of Shrewsbury were from gentry stock, and in Norwich merchants drew on the gentry and yeomen of Norfolk for their apprentices, not on the tradesmen below them. William Mucklowe, a Worcester clothier, whose father was a yeoman and son a country gentleman, exemplifies, albeit in unusually clear and precise detail, what may well have been a familiar feature of the urban social structure. Though towns evidently provided opportunities for social mobility in this period, it was mobility over a relatively short range, and at its most rapid it was more often enjoyed by the recent immigrant than by the established urban family.

Implicit in the pattern described above was that close association between the social élites of town and countryside upon which foreigners often remarked. This was a feature which became more pronounced in the course of the seventeenth century and which had important repercussions for urban society. The entry of gentlemen's sons into urban apprenticeships showed that the gentry had lost any reluctance to put their sons to trade. Although conservative heralds might object, seventeenth century pamphleteers began to give a negative answer to the question posed by one of them: *Whether Apprenticeship Extinguisheth Gentry?* (1629). But this association also contained other, far less beneficial implications for towns, since it threatened in the long run the independence and vitality of urban social life. From at least the sixteenth century the élite of the richest towns had aspired to social acquaintanceship with gentlemen, had hobnobbed with them in social fraternities like the gild of St. George in Norwich, had often accepted them as M.P.s, and always welcomed them as political patrons and residents during the assizes or quarter sessions. By 1600 country gentry were increasingly influential figures on the urban social stage.

These connections were strengthened during the seventeenth century in a number of ways. First, there were the social aspirations of urban rulers themselves, who began to adopt the titles of master and gentleman, whether or not sanctioned by grants of arms: even the leet jury of Manchester and its chief officers were 'gentlemen' by the 1630s. Secondly, there was the growing influence both in taste and attitudes of those professional men, doctors, apothecaries, attorneys, and clergy who were more and more prominent in many larger centres from the Tudor period. By the late seventeenth century they formed a 'pseudo-gentry' class which frequently determined the character of many smaller towns. Thirdly, Restoration towns felt the pressure of large numbers of resident or semi-resident gentry. Thus by 1696 there were well over one hundred gentlemen in Bristol. County towns sometimes succumbed entirely to this gentry dominance. Boston made forty-six noblemen and gentry free in 1634, thus anticipating the action of many other towns, which like Maldon and St. Albans formally acknowledged outside influence in this way during the political crises of the second half of the century. But even the largest and most autonomous of towns saw their rulers aping the habits and tastes of the county gentry and also adopting their claims to social exclusiveness.

However eager this élite might have been to see itself as a 'gentle' ruling class, it was faced for most of our period with the peculiarly urban problems arising from polarization within the social structure. By 1600 poverty was the major concern of all urban governors, not only in decaying towns such as Winchester faced with a long-term decline in employment opportunities, but also in expanding centres like Bristol where commercial crises affected increasingly large numbers of people. The problem had two components. First there were the hard cases of orphan children, old widows, single-parent families, those universally recognized as the deserving poor, who in the past had commonly been granted alms. With the institution of poor relief in sixteenth-century towns the deserving poor formed most of the 4 or 5 per cent of the population which received parish relief. However, during our period the total number of poor was rapidly enlarged by the accession of a second group, the able-bodied poor. These were often men with large families, sometimes new immigrants to a town, sometimes residents who were victims of cyclical unemployment (particularly common in the textile industry). As a result, censuses of the poor often list between a fifth and a third of urban populations as destitute or nearly destitute: 20 per cent of the inhabitants of Worcester were counted as poor in 1556, 25 per cent of the English population of Norwich in 1570, 30 per cent of households in part of Warwick in 1582, a third of the population of one Salisbury parish in 1635. Poverty not infrequently threatened to overwhelm English towns.

The detailed and comprehensive Norwich census of 1570

best illuminates the condition of the urban poor. Nearly half of the men listed were either unskilled labourers or craftsmen in the textile trades, but one third of them were now unemployed. Many were the victims of downward social mobility. Some had once been apprentices who had tried and failed to climb into the freeman class. Others had their own houses but were now faced with mortgage debts. Nevertheless, they strove to make ends meet. A few had their children learning some industrial skills at school. Most secured extra income from their wives and offspring spinning or carding at home. Some women were recorded as helping other women 'in need' with domestic employments, but others had to 'live upon their friends'. A dozen were harlots. The poor were crowded in particular areas of the town. In the two fashionable wards close to the cathedral only 7 or 8 per cent of the population was poor in 1570, but 41 per cent of the inhabitants of St. Giles' parish on the edge of the city were included in the survey. This topographical concentration of the poor presented urban rulers with severe social and police problems, not only through the constant annoyance of begging in the streets and the affrays of the drunk and disorderly, but because of the fear of more organized disturbances. It was no coincidence that the Norwich census was taken after the Appleyard conspiracy, an attempt to incite a popular rising in the town; and those compiling a census of the poor in Ipswich in 1597 reflected the views of all urban magistrates when they noted that the destitute required not only food, fuel, clothes, and tools for their trade, but also 'discipline'.

The motives which inspired the poor relief innovations of English towns in this period were, therefore, by no means altruistic. Nevertheless, magisterial activity in this field is the clearest indication both of the continuing vitality of the ruling élites of urban society and of their responsiveness to changes in the social structure. Following the example set by some continental towns, many English corporations began to regard new mechanisms for the proper care of the poor as an essential mark of urban 'civility'. They initiated experiments with compulsory rating for the relief of the destitute in London, Norwich, York, and Ipswich in the middle decades of the sixteenth century, and they put particular faith and investment into workhouses and houses of correction for the training and isolation of the poor. These institutions were in fashion in the 1570s and 1590s and again in the second decade of the seventeenth century, for example at Leicester, Nottingham, Hull, and Colchester. By the 1620s some corporations, especially those under Puritan influence, were indulging in more costly experiments, establishing municipal brewhouses as in Dorchester and Salisbury, or using the profits from town mills (as at Newcastle-under-Lyme) for the regular support of the poor.

At the same time, the ruling classes of towns were investing even larger sums from their own pockets in charitable endowments for the poor. Research on English philanthropy between 1480 and 1660 has shown that something like three-quarters of all charitable benefactions in the country came from urban donors, with the mercantile élite of towns like London and Bristol taking the lead and the richer men of places as small as Basingstoke quickly following suit. The relief of the poor took up the largest sums, more than half a million pounds being given for this purpose by Londoners, more than £40,000 by the citizens of Bristol before the Restoration. In London alone by 1660 charitable funds ought to have been available to support 17,000 people. This at least was the aspiration and the potential achievement. Yet it is abundantly clear from the Chancery inquisitions into charitable trusts that such funds were often diverted from their intended goal. Corporations sometimes drew on them to tide them over emergencies in civic finance; they misappropriated funds for their own political and patronage purposes; they regularly had difficulty in prising bequests from the clutches of executors. Moreover, while the urban élite might try to salve their consciences by death-bed extravagance, it is also clear that as living members of the ruling class they were often ruthless exploiters of the poor. The census of the Norwich poor, for example, reveals that many of the destitute were lodged in houses belonging to city councillors; thus John Sotherton had packed no less than thirty-four paupers into one of his properties.

The rulers of towns failed to have any decisive impact on the basic problem of poverty. But they gradually became more skilled in dealing with its consequences. They were forced to spend a growing amount of revenue on household relief, and to overcome citizen resistance to the payment of poor rates. Expenditure on poor relief in Exeter and Norwich rose at least ten-fold between the late sixteenth and the later seventeenth centuries. Magistrates also centralized and improved the administration of the poor laws by exercising closer control over parochial officers. In some of the larger cities, where the problem was always massive and time-consuming, magistrates delegated part of the work of regulating relief to separate, specialized authorities. In mid-sixteenth-century London, the five hospitals established after the Reformation were a limited attempt to free the corporation from some of its responsibilities; provincial institutions like Christ's Hospital in Ipswich served a similar function. In 1649 a Corporation of the Poor was founded in the metropolis and other special corporations sprang up in Bristol, Exeter, Norwich, and Hull at the end of the century. New institutions for poor relief were the most striking examples of the growth of civic administration in the seventeenth century.

By 1700, however, the problem of the poor was probably much less critical in most towns than it had been a century before. To some extent this was due to the new effectiveness of the machinery of poor relief, now at last firmly established and accepted after the preceding period of administrative experiment. But the fact that the problem had become more manageable also reflected the growing stabilization of urban populations and the reduction in the earlier high levels of immigration. Only in the largest centres and the new towns did the poor still present a large-scale problem.

The increasingly complex machinery of poor relief gave formal expression to the gulf between the two extremes of the urban social structure and to the attempts of the one side to alleviate the problems and threats presented by the other. Like the array of courts which enforced public order and precedence, the ceremonies of gilds and fellowships, and the polarized residential patterns of towns, it also reinforced the rudimentary consciousness of economic and status divisions which pervaded early modern towns. To talk of 'class' consciousness would be an anachronism. The outbreaks of popular disorder which punctuated urban life were frequently encouraged, and sometimes led, by members of the ruling élite. Evidence of cohesive action along consciously class lines is rare, although seventeenth-century journeymen were combining in Colchester, Exeter, and Worcester in order to raise their wages. Nonetheless, there was a distinct recognition of that evident and growing dichotomy between 'rich' and 'poor'. The author of an attack on the rulers of Thetford in 1577 complained that 'they did more than they might do in . . . dealing with the poor but not with the rich', and the latter feared 'the animating of the inferior people' in consequence. A Norwich cobbler thought the imposition of sumptuary regulations on labourers and journeymen in 1554 was no more than an attempt by the élite 'to pick quarrels with poor men. But poor men will speak one day'. The distinction between the 'richer sort' and the 'inferior', 'common', or 'poorer sort' was as commonplace in urban court records as the related emphasis on the concepts of 'order' and 'rule'.

For much of our period then, the social structure of many English towns had suffered intense strain, with a growing and open polarization between an increasingly pampered, narrow élite and the large army of destitute poor tramping the streets. But by the last decades of the seventeenth century it is likely that these social stresses had been contained. At the bottom end of urban society the problem of the poor had at last come under control—at least in most older centres. Nearer the top of the urban social order, the élite had been stabilized and sometimes enlarged by an accession of county gentry and professional men, less concerned with the social divisions within the small town and more aware of social developments in a wider, national context.

9

The Political Order

THE political life and activity of many early modern towns was dominated and to a large extent determined by the charters and royal grants which gave them their privileges and independent existence. Charters defined the structure of urban politics both internally and externally: on the one hand the shape of the civic élite and its powers over the citizenry; on the other, the relationship between towns and outside authorities, local and national. The period 1500–1700 saw continuous disputes and conflict in both political areas. As a result, urban rulers spent much of their time trying to obtain new charters or confirm controversial clauses in old ones. For its part, the central government quickly appreciated the political possibilities inherent in its freedom to refuse or accede to these local demands. By 1600 it was taking the initiative and using its powers to interfere directly in urban politics in order to achieve wider political and parliamentary ends. The chartered rights which towns had seen as guarantees of their autonomy had by the late seventeenth century become pawns in a large and complex political game which eventually eroded the independence of all but the great cities.

This does not mean, of course, that unchartered towns had no significant political life of their own, though in the absence of corporation records it is often difficult to get a clear idea of their development. As we saw earlier, numerous market-towns were hardly distinguishable legally from villages: in theory they were ruled by manorial lords through courts leet and baron presided over by the lord's steward. Some, but not all, had achieved grants of rudimentary borough rights, burgesses, and a borough court (as in the case of Leeds after

1207), or had acquired a gild merchant which co-operated
with the manorial court (as in Totnes at the start of our
period). But even in the simplest of these towns it is often
possible to recognize the existence of an informal political
structure increasingly dominated by the richer inhabitants.
This might be centred on the parish vestry, as in Birmingham
where the parish was independent enough to engage in
prolonged disputes with the county quarter sessions during
the seventeenth century. Influence could also be exerted by
feoffees or trustees of local charitable endowments as at
Bicester, or through the administration of a workhouse as at
Halifax after 1635. Even the seigneurial apparatus might be
infiltrated: as was the case in Tudor Lewes, for example,
where, although courts and markets were in the hands of the
lord, day-to-day management of the town was said to be
controlled by 'a society of the wealthier and discreeter sort of
Townsmen commonly called the Twelve . . . [who] upon
death or removal are supplied by the election of the greater
number of the subsisting society'. As we have already seen,
courts leet themselves could develop into relatively sophisticated machines for local government. In Taunton the
Bishop of Winchester's manorial court was ruled by a jury of
richer inhabitants who appointed more than thirty local
officials a year. These towns, even without the benefits of
corporation charters, were clearly producing oligarchies of
their own. And in some cases the oligarchy pulled itself up by
its boot-laces to full parity with its equivalent in longer-
established towns: thus the merchants of Leeds successively
bought the presentation to the vicarage, a charter of incorporation (1626), and finally the remaining manorial rights
over the town.

But it is the chartered boroughs of later medieval England
which present more definite and better-documented evidence
of the politics of the early modern town. Already many towns
enjoyed an enormous and complex variety of medieval rights
and privileges. But for most of them, full incorporation
served as the ultimate accolade, giving their rulers the status
of representatives of the whole community in judicial and
financial matters. The classic age for the incorporation of

boroughs occurred in the two centuries after 1440 and the movement was given additional impetus, as in the case of Warwick in 1545, by the civic desire to share in the secularization of church lands. Between 1500 and 1700 no less than 160 English towns received charters of incorporation, two-thirds of them before 1600. In the same period many towns secured their own justices of the peace and quarter sessions, and some of the largest of them also acquired the final mark of autonomy, county status itself. As in the less sophisticated urban communities, however, the dominant theme, the driving force behind these aspirations and the consequence of their achievement, was the growth of oligarchy.

Charters of incorporation have been described as 'tools of an irresistible tendency towards exclusiveness'. They were the treaties of alliance between a Crown which wished to see power in the hands of a group small and rich enough to be answerable to it, and urban élites determined to perpetuate their local status. By James I's reign the Crown's interest in closed oligarchies was precisely exemplified in the detailed arrangements for new towns in the Ulster plantation. But in 1512 it was already a precept in Court circles, expressed in relation to disputes in Nottingham, that 'if you shall suffer the commons to rule and follow their appetite and desire, farewell all good order'. For their part the wealthy élite of towns would always concur with the magistrates of Gloucester in 1584: 'Experience hath taught us what a difficult thing it hath always been to deal in any matter where the multitude of burgesses have voice.' In many towns there had been pressure during the fifteenth century from commons and freemen for a greater say in municipal politics. But beginning with the parliamentary statute of 1489 which regulated the government of Leicester and Northampton, this pressure was regularly and simply bought off by the provision of an additional, larger council. In theory consulted by the élite, these second councils rarely controlled its actions. At Worcester, for example, the second Council of Forty Eight served as no more than a 'docile substitute for genuine public participation in city government'. In Stamford the rule of the First and Second 'Twelves' completely overshadowed the more popular Third Twelve.

During the sixteenth century the large Common Councils at York, King's Lynn, Norwich, and London increasingly lost control of civic administration to aldermanic cliques which met more frequently and had added to their old civic status by their new prestigious and powerful positions as justices of the peace. By the end of the century small, closed councils with members sitting for life and able to co-opt one another were, with few exceptions, the usual means of government in English towns.

This development had, of course, strong local roots, both formal and informal. Oligarchies had important links with particular religious gilds and craft fellowships, which were themselves developing exclusive ruling groups in the sixteenth century. The Trinity Gilds at Coventry and Worcester, the St. Katherine's Gild at Stamford, and that of St. George at Norwich, were social clubs for the élite, while the oligarchies were supported in Tudor London, Exeter, and Newcastle by their close identification with the Merchant Adventurers. Ruling cliques were also bound together by marriage and family ties, like the aldermen and jurats of Dover who were said in 1632 to be 'all linked together in kindred, uncle and cousin'. In Elizabeth's reign the mayors of Leicester were drawn from only twenty-six interrelated families. One third of the Elizabethan aldermen of London were related to other aldermen and the aldermen's court was dominated by a cluster of only fifteen important families. These oligarchies naturally exerted careful control over their own recruitment, sometimes even establishing clear economic criteria for membership: candidates for election as aldermen of London, for instance, had to have properrty worth £1,333 in 1525, £10,000 in 1640.

At the same time, oligarchy was also a response to the real demands of local government. With the growth of civic administration, particularly during the sixteenth century, there was an increasing need for a powerful standing committee which might take decisions about the day-to-day conduct of civic government without recourse to the wordy debate of corporate councils. The aldermanic bench was the obvious candidate for this role. At Northampton, for instance, during the 1580s we find the mayor and aldermen increasingly meeting once a week, 'to consult about public affairs' and 'see the people brought in good obedience'.

The growth of oligarchy also reflected another civic development. Because of heavier administrative responsibilities and the rapid rate of sixteenth-century inflation, civic expenditure rose sharply. This was at a time when many corporate towns faced serious economic instability and the contraction of their old established industries and trades, often a main source of civic income. The result was serious and sometimes acute corporate indebtedness. At Gloucester, for instance, civic finance plunged into deficit during the early years of Elizabeth's reign and by 1574–5 out-payments were more than twice the town's annual receipts. At Leicester the situation was less acute, but deficits were recurrent throughout Elizabeth's reign. There were similar problems at Sandwich, Warwick, Hastings, and Southampton. In consequence, towns had to rely heavily on short-term loans from their civic leaders. At Gloucester the corporation only managed to keep afloat financially because the four incoming city stewards (or chamberlains) advanced the city enough money to pay off its previous year's deficit. Elsewhere mayors and other civic officials regularly had to meet small-scale expenditure out of their own pockets. Insistence on wealthy office-holders was not only a matter of upper-class choice but of civic necessity. The point was underlined by the rising number of substantial men who showed themselves unwilling to bear the high costs of civic service. Nonetheless, most towns managed to fill their corporate offices with members of the economic élite, even if generous rewards were needed as inducement. At Southampton, for instance, it was evident in 1573 that the mercantile élite, those burgesses 'as do use and occupy sciences and faculties', ruled the town to the exclusion of 'men of occupations, artificers and handicraftsmen who seldom or never attain within this town to that wealth and ability to bear the said offices'.

The growth of oligarchic power was emphasized by other developments. First, there was the disappearance of many traditional expressions of the coherence of the urban community. The great religious processions of the later medieval town had provided regular occasions for bringing together different layers of the civic hierarchy. After the Reformation these were abolished or phased out, and the civic ceremony which survived was oriented in a different direction. Processions of aldermen and councillors to church or court, for example, proclaimed the status of the ruling oligarchy rather than the unity of the community as a whole. They were characterized by new and elaborate civic insignia, mayoral maces and swords of state, symbols of the authority of urban magistrates. Such public displays did nothing to disguise the growing emphasis on private politics and secret decision-making within the élite. At Hastings, after 1603, mayoral elections took place not in public but in the court hall, and by 1622 the Council of Twenty-Four at Winchester was well aware that it was not 'made acquainted with the affairs of the city . . . as far forth as the mayor and his brethren'. The stress on secrecy in civic politics was constantly reiterated in town minute-books and it was reflected too in the erection or rebuilding of many town guildhalls, often with private rooms for the aldermanic clique.

The Reformation not only swept a good deal of civic ritual and public politics off the streets, but it also dealt a blow at the importance of the old craft fraternities. In the late Middle Ages these had often served as subsidiary centres of political power, complementing the authority of the corporate hierarchy headed by the mayor and aldermen. However, in the late sixteenth century the gilds were strictly regulated and supervised by the civic rulers: they became organs of civic government and instruments of oligarchic control.

The authority of the oligarchy was further enhanced by the expansion of the adminstrative machinery in many towns. The poor laws, in particular, led to the appearance of a large number of new parish officials—beadles, overseers, and the like. These came under the control of the ruling élite, especially in those towns where the latter wielded power as justices of the peace. At sessions the aldermanic justices also supervised highway surveyors and constables, as well as exercising the many other administrative duties imposed on them by the Tudor monarchy. It was not simply that extra authority accrued to the ruling clique through their position as magistrates. The bench of J.P.s, by the mid-seventeenth century often the dominant administrative organ in towns, was more obviously independent of communal control than the traditional civic courts with their powerful, if socially select, juries.

The new administrative authority of the ruling élite was supported in the late sixteenth century by the rise of a primitive form of civic bureaucracy. Of course, town clerks had been fairly active in most major towns during the medieval period, but they now acquired new power and importance. As often as not they were prominent county attorneys and men of substantial landed status. With their retinue of clerks they were busy and influential members of the civic polity. In Caroline Liverpool the town clerk, Robert Dobson, was clearly a powerful figure in his own right, and one or two town clerks of the Kentish boroughs aspired to similar status. By the mid-seventeenth century the town clerk was often the lynch-pin of civic administration.

Another pillar of oligarchic politics in the sixteenth and seventeenth centuries was corruption. Favourable leases of corporation property; loans from corporation and charitable funds; the power as magistrate to regulate urban economic life to one's own advantage as merchant or employer; the use of civic office to blackmail one's enemies and opponents; the opportunity to peculate the city's petty cash: all these were among the common perquisites of civic office. One might well argue that the fruits of office had to be high because of the heavy political and financial responsibilities of the office-holders. Up to a point this is certainly true, but there can be little doubt that civic corruption also served to consolidate and buttress oligarchic power. Complaints by ordinary citizens that they were unable to obtain justice in civic courts because of magisterial chicanery are a commonplace in records of the period, and undoubtedly served to bring local courts and town government into popular disrepute.

Not surprisingly, conflicts between oligarchies and ordinary citizens dominated the political life of towns for much of the period, with charges of secret government and corruption well to the fore. We find disputes of this sort at small market-towns like High Wycombe and Woodstock as well as larger corporate centres like Nottingham, Warwick, and Canterbury. Tension was particularly acute during the 1590s when high prices and high taxation caused a groundswell of protest at Leicester, Norwich, St. Albans, Sandwich, Doncaster, and Colchester. Oligarchic mismanagement of town lands was usually the most inflammatory issue: thus at Nottingham it was alleged that the corporation had 'taken the best ground to the richest men and let poor men have nothing.' On occasion the leaders were relative newcomers to the town unable to break into the corridors of power. At Faversham after 1610, opposition to the oligarchy was led by men who had arrived there in the last ten years. In Maldon in the 1590s recently arrived freemen expressed their frustration by creating 'a counterfeit corporation' in rivalry to the established regime.

In general, however, these assaults failed to curtail the power of the oligarchy. Usually they merely hardened the magistrates' resolve and led to further restrictions on the commons' involvement in politics, even at the lowest, ward level. The basic problem was that even small traders and burgesses, the rank and file of opposition, were frightened that disorder might get out of hand: they did not want to be engulfed by disturbances among labourers, apprentices, or the immigrant poor. True, alliances were sometimes formed between discontented freemen and the unprivileged towns-folk below them. Such combinations may have been behind the riots against the enclosure of the Nottingham and York common-fields in the early sixteenth century, and the 1633 disorders at Newcastle. But these cases were exceptional. The freemen's fear of popular anarchy may also have militated against those coalitions of burgesses and peasants which dominated French popular disturbances in the seventeenth century. Thus, we know only of the commons of Beverley and York who joined the Pilgrimage of Grace after a period of growing antagonism towards their merchant oligarchies, and of the citizens of Norwich who sympathized with Ket and the

Norfolk rebels. More often, the small traders who served as constables and watchmen stamped on threats like that presented by one man in London in 1549, found 'enticing men's servants and apprentices to go with him to the rebels at Norwich'.

Yet if the unrest caused by civic oligarchy had only limited repercussions on the internal politics of towns, the implications for their relations with the political world outside were much more serious. From the start most town oligarchies relied heavily on outside support, particularly that of the Crown, and this was increased rather than diminished by domestic discontent. The Tudor regime, ever-concerned to extend its provincial authority, exploited the opportunity to the full. In Kent and Norfolk, for instance, the Crown repeatedly interfered in municipal affairs from the 1570s. Royal intervention reached its climax in the 1590s when the government's fiscal and military needs drove it to widespread invasions of corporate rights.

Nor was the Crown the only beneficiary from the political instability within towns. As often as not the Crown's agents were county gentry or county lawyers. The royal commissioners who investigated the political faction and oligarchic corruption at New Romney in the 1580s were all leading local magnates, who thereby acquired an indirect influence over town business. The same men, presiding over county quarter sessions, made further incursions on municipal autonomy. In this connection it is significant that numerous sixteenth-century towns began to appoint recorders, often prominent lawyers and county justices, who voiced royal and county points of view to the detriment of civic independence.

Many town magistrates, in fact, went out of the way to cultivate the support of county magnates. In this way they consolidated their own position while saving the town from the worst effects of Crown and gentry interference. Leases, gifts, and other *douceurs* were liberally dispensed to win outside favours, while parliamentary elections in towns were progressively dominated by county magnates or their nominees. The creation or restoration of seventy parliamentary boroughs in the sixteenth century was mainly the result of pressure from the gentry for more openings into political life at the centre. We can see the same pressure at work in the Wentworths' calculated sponsorship of the restoration of Pontefract in 1621. It is true that the gentry's growing control of borough seats was far from absolute. Large towns like Bristol, Newcastle, and York could still afford to keep control of their elections. The swings and roundabouts of national politics also left boroughs with occasional room for manoeuvre: thus the fall of the Duke of Norfolk in 1570 liberated Great Yarmouth from aristocratic domination. Nonetheless, in general, the gentry overshadowed borough representation from the sixteenth century.

Not surprisingly, as competition for seats developed, parliamentary elections became entangled in the political conflict within towns between magistrates and commonalty. In the parliamentary contests in Warwick in the 1580s the Dudleys supported the popular, Puritan party which was also opposing the oligarchy in municipal politics. They further raised the issue of the size of the electorate, threatening to invoke the rights of the commonalty to vote. In certain towns by 1600 we can already see, in embryo at least, opposing alliances of Court magnates and town oligarchies on the one hand, and more radical gentry and town commons on the other.

The issue of the size of the electorate now became a dominant theme of constituency politics in boroughs where the Tudor triumph of oligarchy had in practice reserved the choice of M.P.s to the mayor and his close colleagues. When after 1604 the House of Commons was able to determine cases of disputed elections, it quickly began to favour larger electorates. This was especially evident during the politically disturbed 1620s, as can be seen in the cases of Sandwich and Chippenham. The same decade also saw the pressure of frequent elections and the organization of Puritan factions among the freemen push numerous towns in a similar direction: at Exeter, Warwick, and Colchester the franchise was consequently extended beyond the oligarchy. Moreover, in places like Reading, Nottingham, and Hythe there were signs that urban rulers were giving way to pressure from below and resisting the nomination of M.P.s from outside. By 1630 the majority of parliamentary boroughs had large electorates which the urban oligarchy could not ignore.

The incorporation of municipal politics into the national political arena had serious implications for the relationship between towns and the central government. As municipalities threatened to become more radical, the central government showed itself increasingly hostile to urban interests. When disputes occurred between bishops and corporations, as at Salisbury, Chichester, and York, the Caroline Privy Council favoured the episcopal position. Likewise, the proposed incorporation of the London suburbs in 1636 showed the Crown's lack of faith in the political institutions of the capital. A letter to Archbishop Laud in 1640, commenting on the recent incorporation of Sunderland, a town dominated by the Lilburnes, reflected the change of attitude in Court circles:

> 'It is an honour to the kingdom to have such towns . . . to come up and flourish from small beginnings. But . . . the King's Majesty had better for a while despise that honour and profit that accrues to him that way . . . than to suffer little towns to grow big and anti-monarchy to boot; for where are all these pestilent nests of Puritans hatched but in corporations, where they swarm and breed like hornets.'

Faced by mistrust at Court and popular pressure from below, municipal oligarchies were in a weak and exposed position on the eve of the Civil War.

It is a remarkable testimony to the powerful forces working for oligarchy both inside and outside towns that the framework of select government nevertheless survived the crises of the next twenty years. It was shaken on more than one occasion. The parliamentary elections of 1640 gave fresh opportunities in towns like Abingdon, Salisbury, and Bewdley for attacks on the oligarchy and attempts to enlarge the franchise, sometimes in conjunction with assaults on the machinery of the Eleven Years Tyranny. In the following years the royalist stance of many urban élites encouraged agitation and change from below, best exemplified by the seizure of power from Lord Mayor Gurney and his royalist aldermen by the Common Council of London in 1641–2. But here, as elsewhere, municipal government was only temporarily or marginally broadened. Royalist aldermen might be purged in Bristol, Newcastle, York, and Norwich in the course of, or immediately after, the Civil War, but their successors were wealthy men already close to and aspiring to inclusion in the inner ring. Henry Dawson's friends, who took over Newcastle in 1645, included fewer Hostmen and Mercers than the pre-1642 élite but they were still men of substance. There were genuine experiments in more open government only at High Wycombe and Bedford, which gained a 'levelling constitution' temporarily subjecting municipal officers to popular election by the freemen. There were some moves to reduce civic corruption and improve the functioning of town courts. Otherwise change was minimal. Political upheaval at the centre and popular opposition to high taxation and extreme religious radicalism in many towns maintained the government's interest in preserving a malleable oligarchy, while the new civic rulers were just as determined to consolidate their power as their predecessors. In Norwich the purged corporation of 1649 was as opposed as ever to 'popular elections' which were 'continually disquiet, factious, and perilous', while the radical Barrington faction in Colchester obtained a new, more exclusive charter in 1656 because the old one gave 'too great a power . . . to the people to slight the magistracy of the place'.

This failure to broaden the bases of political power in towns in the 1640s and 1650s, and the consequent continued lack of political unity, was probably a major reason why towns did not exert any formative influence on the Revolution—despite the promise held out by several of the developments of the 1620s and some of the elections of 1640. The attitude of urban élites remained essentially defensive, although there were, of course, exceptions. The Puritan magistrates of Gloucester inspired the citizenry to a famous defence against the royalist siege there in 1643, and subsequently played a prominent part in the Parliamentary cause in the West. Many inhabitants of Birmingham, Coventry, and Manchester

were also firm and militant opponents of the cavaliers in the
1640s. Not least important, popular radicalism in London
had, as we know, a vital impact on parliamentary events
during the decade, though it is significant here that the city
as a whole was increasingly divided, and in the final analysis
the London radicals lost out to the generals of the army.
Certainly most other towns were much more passive. Change
was often imposed upon them from outside, by military force
in the Civil War as with the disastrous sack of Leicester in
1645, or the use of military governors as in Yarmouth under
the Eastern Association, or by the gradual loss of political
authority to the county, such as happened at Chester in the
1650s. Many towns eagerly seized the opportunity to pick up
the confiscated property of bishops, deans, and chapters.
Lincoln, York, and other towns expanded their jurisdiction
by taking over former cathedral liberties. Aylesbury, with the
support of Thomas Scot and the Rump Parliament, bought
its freedom from the manorial court in 1650. Yet while the
Revolution brought some rewards for civic acquiescence,
there was also increasing central interference. In 1649 the
Rump had set up a committee for corporations, and in 1652
with the prospect of new parliamentary elections it was
instructed to call in all charters. The Rump's dissolution
occurred before much progress could be made. But the
manipulation of corporations through the revision of charters
now became a continuing theme of urban politics, as we can
see at Salisbury and Colchester under the Protectorate where
the new grants nominated the mayor and aldermen and
defined and consolidated a closed oligarchy. The governments of the Interregnum refined tools of influence and
control which provided a precedent for the later Stuarts.

By 1660 successive purges and new charters had created
considerable confusion in the ruling élites of numerous towns
such as Reading. But this was simply the prelude to much
more drastic change. After the Restoration the commissioners
appointed under the Corporation Act remodelled the corporations of many towns. In Reading itself, in Gloucester,
Newcastle-under-Lyme, Leicester, and Shrewsbury, more
than half the councillors were expelled. In the years after

1663 some of those excluded crept back into municipal power in towns like Leicester and Colchester and contributed to the Whig and dissenting successes at the time of the Exclusion Crisis. However, this was only a temporary interlude and a succession of *quo warranto* attacks on corporation charters completed the disruption of urban politics. Between 1681 and 1686, 119 new corporation charters imposed Tory dominance. These changes were sometimes in line with the local revival of Anglican interests, apparent in towns like Norwich and Bristol before 1681. But outside interference was the dominant force and it achieved its climax in the thirty-five new charters of 1687–8 by which James II swung the pendulum against the Tory interest in his attempt to construct an alliance between Dissent and Roman Catholicism. By 1689 the personnel and records of many boroughs were in complete disarray and the confusion of charters and magistrates persisted in towns like Chester and Wilton well into the next century.

Although they have yet to be fully explored, the rapid changes of the 1680s clearly had some connections with the structure of politics within towns, with the older conflicts between oligarchy and freemen, and with local disputes over the size of the electorate. There was no uniform pattern, however, since the content of the charters reflected the government's interests and these varied from town to town. In Leicester in 1684 the franchise was extended from the corporation to all who paid scot and lot (local rates) because this was thought to favour the Tory interest; by contrast the same year saw the free burgesses of Colchester stripped of their old municipal power and the purged oligarchy was in future to recruit itself by co-option. Other traditional themes of urban politics also reappeared. In Nottingham the mayor welcomed the chance to increase the size of the council to allow in deserving aspirants and 'the better to exclude the rest', the *rationale* of many conciliar changes in the later fifteenth century. Election disputes in Lancaster in James II's reign between loyalist and Monmouth candidates revived older quarrels between 'the governing party and the common freemen, and particularly betwixt the drapers and hatters'.

But here the vital influence was that of the country gentry who had their 'servants and attendants' enrolled as freemen and overawed the burgesses with two companies of the militia. For the continuing development in urban politics most encouraged in the 1680s was the intervention of outsiders, gentry representatives of the newly dominant county community. The 1688 charter intruded aldermen into Warwick from adjacent Catholic rural areas; the Leicester charter of 1684 made the Earl of Huntingdon Recorder as an instrument of royal control. In small towns like Wells the early 1680s saw the introduction of gentlemen as freemen and magistrates. Even at prosperous Liverpool there was a determined attempt to subordinate the town to the shire. This reached its humiliating climax on 8 April 1685 when the deputy mayor and the freemen had to trek out to Bewsey Hall to receive the grant of a revised charter from the Crown's mayoral nominee, the country Tory, Sir Richard Atherton.

For most of our period, therefore, the politics of urban communities were dominated by the establishment of oligarchy and the vulnerability that came with it. In order to survive, civic oligarchies relied heavily on royal support and on powerful political patrons at Court and in the countryside. This in turn led to growing outside interference and disruption, particularly in electoral politics. In the short-run the rise of oligarchy also had serious consequences for the internal stability of towns with domestic dissension and unrest chiming in with national political divisions, especially during the early seventeenth century. Yet it would be wrong to exaggerate. As we have seen, another important development of the period was the growing power and effectiveness of civic administration with its own small bureaucracy. In the late seventeenth century this was often operating relatively efficiently without close supervision from above. By 1700 one has the impression that for all the noisy party strife and confusion within chartered corporations there was never any real risk of a collapse of public order. The administrative stability of the English town had come to stay.

The Cultural Role

WE have so far examined four of the prominent features of early modern towns—their demographic, economic, social, and political structures. We must finally consider the more elusive but no less important cultural characteristics which helped both to define their image and identity and to determine the nature of their influence on society at large.

Townsmen certainly thought of themselves as representatives of civilization and sophistication in comparison with the rude and backward countryside. Towns after all were islands of 'civility' in a sea of rural 'rusticity'. The lawyers and their clerks at Canterbury for instance sneered at the ignorance and inarticulateness of their country clients; while in Henry Porter's *Two Angry Women of Abington* (1599) a townswoman is reprimanded with: 'What will the neighbouring country vulgar say/When as they hear that you fell out at dinner?' Contemporary literature abounds in explicit contrasts between the habits, language, and dress of uncivilized countryfolk and those of their educated urban neighbours.

It is difficult to assess how far these literary stereotypes conformed to reality, however. In some respects there were evident differences in popular behaviour between town and country. Not only did respectable townsmen try to avoid the country dialect of the peasants, but with their fancy clothes they out-dressed the latter too. As a result of the growth of internal trade and conspicuous consumption during the sixteenth century, urban dress—always more elaborate than that of countryfolk—became increasingly sophisticated, following the helter-skelter of fashion. Even in the sixteenth century, London set the trend. By the mid-seventeenth century, with its increasing economic and social influence, the capital (led by the Court) was the couturier to the kingdom. Periwigs, ribbons, Brandenburg coats, and waistcoats all travelled post-haste down from London to grace the substantial figures of provincial society.

We know less about other patterns of urban behaviour. It is possible that formal civility and conspicuous consumption in towns were accompanied, as we noted earlier, by greater anonymity in social relationships. The rapid growth of London and its high turnover of population may have led to that impersonality which is said to have occurred in some great continental cities in the sixteenth and seventeenth centuries and which we usually associate with the modern metropolis. But the evidence for this is not wholly convincing. Certainly there are numerous indications of more customary, more traditional attitudes and values in both large and small English towns at this time. Face-to-face relationships and rural concepts of neighbourliness may have been preserved, for example, in separate streets and quarters of towns which were often dominated by a single occupational group. The continuing appeal of magic to urban as well as rural residents also suggests that in some respects at least behaviour patterns in town and countryside were alike.

Nevertheless, the physical size and complexity of towns, and the variety of the religious and educational institutions which they contained, undoubtedly gave urban life a quality quite distinct from that of the countryside. While we cannot measure urban patterns of behaviour and popular attitudes with any exactitude, we can point to the potential influence of these more concrete phenomena and to their wider impact on society outside the towns. The dominant image presented by towns in late medieval England was that provided by the medium-sized city or borough. Physically this meant an urban community surrounded by an impressive circuit of town walls, its sky-line decorated by a host of churches, monasteries, hospitals, and craft-halls. York was rather exceptional with its surfeit of public or quasi-public buildings, including the Minster, St. Mary's Abbey, thirty-three parish churches, St. Anthony's Hall, St. William's College, the

Merchant Tailors' Hall, and the splendid Guildhall. But even a comparatively small community like Dover could muster four parish churches, a monastery, two hospitals, and the usual town walls. For the migrant labourer or the country-man bringing his chickens or eggs to market the sheer profusion of large civic buildings, often built in stone, must have been both awesome and exhilarating, in contrast to the mainly small-scale, wattle-and-daub constructions of the countryside.

No less impressive to the outsider was the complex street pattern of the established town. In the oldest centres like Lincoln, Exeter, and Chester the main roads roughly adhered to the lines of the Roman city: at Chester they crossed more or less at right angles in the town centre. In some of the new towns of the twelfth and thirteenth centuries such as Salisbury there was a regular grid-iron layout, the street plan having been designed by the town's founder. Elsewhere, however, the layout was usually more irregular. At Southampton (see figure 2), the principal thoroughfare was English Street, stretching north–south through the town: joining this, in a somewhat random fashion, east–west, were several other main streets—Simnel Street, West Street, and East Street (leading through the Eastgate to the important suburb of St. Mary's). Behind the main streets were numerous second-ary lanes and alleys that honeycombed the town, many of them changing direction and even name from one generation to the next.

However, the image and reputation of the established town in the late Middle Ages did not rely simply on its impressive physical appearance. Another central motif was the richness of its cultural life. One of the more important elements here was civic ceremonial and pageantry. At Canterbury, for in-stance, the principal event of the civic calendar was the annual procession on the Eve of the Translation of St. Thomas à Becket (6 July), when a series of floats or tableaux burrowed its way through the many narrow streets of the city. Each float depicted a famous religious event, such as the Nativity, the Assumption, and—the procession's splendid centrepiece—the Martyrdom of Becket himself. Although the

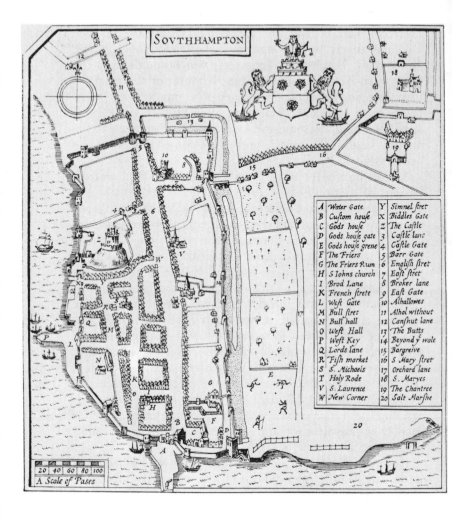

SOVTHHAMPTON

A	Water Gate	Y	Simnel ſtret
B	Cuſtom houſe	X	Biddles Gate
C	Gods houſe	Z	The Caſtle
D	Gods houſe gate	3	Caſtle lane
E	Gods houſe grene	4	Caſtle Gate
F	The Friers	5	Barr Gate
G	The Friers Rum	6	Engliſh ſtret
H	S Iohns church	7	Eaſt ſtret
I	Brod Lane	8	Broker lane
K	French ſtrete	9	Eaſt Gate
L	Weſt Gate	10	Alhallowes
M	Bull ſtret	11	Alhal without
N	Bull hall	12	Canſhut lane
O	Weſt Hall	13	The Butts
P	Weſt Key	14	Beyond ý wale
Q	Lords lane	15	Bargreive
R	Fiſh market	16	S Mary ſtret
S	S. Michaels	17	Orchard lane
T	Holy Rode	18	S. Maryes
V	S. Laurence	19	The Chantree
W	New Corner	20	Salt Marſhe

20 40 60 80 100
A Scale of Paſes

central theme was religious, the ceremony also had a clear civic dimension since the procession was headed by a large force of city archers and bill-men, while the mayor and aldermen in full regalia brought up the rear. In smaller towns urban pageantry was inevitably on a less splendid scale, but many communities like Beverley, New Romney, and Wakefield, staged well-known mystery plays, often at Whitsuntide, which reflected both civic and religious consciousness.

We noted earlier the important political role played by ceremony in towns, demonstrating as it did the formal unity and cohesion of the urban polity. But processions and plays also had a wider importance. To the large numbers of countryfolk who thronged to town to watch the pageantry, or who saw the plays when they came on tour to the villages of the urban hinterland, these urban spectacles were an impressive exhibition of the pride and reputation of a particular community. They thus underlined a town's cultural ties with the neighbouring countryside. At Lincoln the organizers of the pageants of St. Anne's gild even borrowed some of the actors' costumes from county landowners.

A more continuous element in the cultural function of the late medieval town was afforded by the Church. The concentration of religious activity in most established urban settlements, often with an array of shrines and relics, attracted the pilgrimages, prayers, and legacies of the peasantry almost to the eve of the Reformation. Admittedly, some of the urban shrines in the south-east, like that at Canterbury, were in decay by the later fifteenth century, but those in other parts of the country, such as Norfolk, were probably doing a good trade right up to the Dissolution. Not surprisingly the image of the relevant saint often figured prominently in civic regalia.

Southampton from a map by John Speed (1611). The lay-out is fairly typical of many larger towns at this time: the straggling suburbs of St. Mary's and All Saints Without, inhabited by the very poor; the fortifications (now rather decayed); the five parish churches; the markets and merchant houses near the centre. The leading thoroughfare was English Street where the houses were reportedly 'fair, neat, beautiful, straight and handsome' and where the new market-house (576) stood by St. Lawrence's church. Part of the open area within the walls was doubtless occupied, as elsewhere, by orchards and gardens, but some probably lay derelict, as a result of the decay of the Tudor port owing to London competiton.

Religion was closely connected with another aspect of the cultural role of pre-Reformation towns, education. Although the great age of the schools established by religious orders had been the fourteenth century, many urban monasteries as well as the non-monastic cathedrals continued to provide some instruction for townsfolk and country boys at the start of the sixteenth century. At the market-town of Dartford, for instance, a house of Dominican nuns taught the sons and daughters of neighbouring gentlefolk, and in Bury St. Edmunds, Evesham, and Reading the abbeys supported schools in the town. In addition chantry priests frequently initiated small groups of young town children in the elements of basic literacy. The fifteenth century saw the beginnings of endowed schools founded by laymen, but in 1500 education was still overwhelmingly dominated by the Church.

The Church thus had a central role in shaping the image and wider influence of most urban centres in the later Middle Ages. As a result the Reformation, which moved steadily across the kingdom from the 1530s and which attracted early support in a number of towns, had a dramatic, sometimes devastating effect. Not least important was its impact on the physical appearance of many larger communities through the damage inflicted by the Dissolution of the Monasteries in the later 1530s, and the suppression of the colleges and chantries a decade later. A number of religious houses were converted into the town mansions of prosperous merchants, county gentry, or Tudor adminstrators. The White Friars at Coventry, for example, became the town house of that rising Edwardian bureaucrat, John Hales. But many others fell into permanent decay, their rubble carted off to build private houses or royal fortresses and their sites left derelict for generations. As early as 1540 a parliamentary statute for the rebuilding of Norwich, Canterbury, and other major cities complained that they 'now are fallen down, decayed and at this day remain unreedified, and do lie as desolate and vacant grounds'. The Protestant attack on the old religious fabric even extended to the multiplicity of parish churches in certain towns. Many were judged redundant and demolished.

Lincoln, for example, lost more than half its parish churches between the 1530s and the 1550s.

Of course the Reformation was not the only factor affecting the urban landscape in this period. With the progressive extension of Tudor peace and order across the kingdom, the town wall began to lose it former military value and was often allowed to decay: this was a parallel development to the no less significant rise in the importance of wall-less market-towns as representatives of urban society in the sixteenth century. By the early 1600s, town walls rarely provided any effective barrier against outsiders. When towns tried to use them to establish a *cordon sanitaire* against plague, infected incomers were able to infiltrate the town without trouble. It was, however, the Civil War which saw the final ruin of many town walls. Hastily repaired to withstand the assault of royalist or parliamentarian armies, they were often badly damaged during the fighting or were subsequently slighted—either by Parliament as at Canterbury, or by the Restoration regime in the case of Gloucester and Coventry. Nor was the damage inflicted by the Civil War confined to the walls of towns. Other public buildings, especially churches, also suffered badly in the fighting, as at Scarborough and Torrington, where a powder magazine stored in the church blew up with devastating effect.

Everything would indicate that public building suffered a notable eclipse in most English towns during the sixteenth and seventeenth centuries. Apart from the erection of almshouses and the occasional grammar school or church, the only major new constructions were town-halls and market-crosses. There were new or rebuilt town-halls in places like Abingdon, Aylesbury, Guildford, Leicester, and Gravesend—monuments to the rise of closed civic government. Even so they were rarely ambitious constructions: most were small and cramped, fitting surroundings, one might say, for the oligarchies which met in them. Rather more splendid were the market-crosses or market-houses established or enlarged to cater for the rapid growth of internal trade. At Exeter there were special buildings erected for the cloth and yarn markets.

Otherwise the main emphasis in the early modern town moved from public to private building. Although the early Tudor period had probably seen a slump in the urban property market, by 1600 new or enlarged houses were springing up in many centres. On the outskirts of larger towns, often outside the old town walls, the traveller met an ugly sprawl of tenements, converted barns, and crude shacks, housing the growing number of immigrant poor. At Southampton even the gates and towers in the walls, once the city's pride, were turned into temporary shelters for the impoverished. By contrast, inside the walls, often in the more central or salubrious parts of town, the prosperous merchants improved their mansions, adding extra rooms and fashionable refinements like glass-windows, fireplaces and panelling. Also near the centre of town, medieval hostelries were enlarged and new inns founded to cope with the development of local trade and the growing number of travellers, both gentry and merchants. Frequently they were the largest buildings in town, with extensive frontages, a multitude of guest-rooms ranged round large courtyards, and accommodation for a considerable number of horses and coaches. In Salisbury alone, in 1686, there were reported to be 548 beds for visitors and stables for 865 horses, while in Exeter in 1671 only the great houses in the cathedral close could compare with the city's inns in the number of hearths they contained. At the end of our period, Daniel Defoe declared that The George at Northampton was 'more like a palace than an inn'.

The seventeenth century also saw the general appearance in towns of brick-built houses with tiled roofs, instead of the timbered and thatched constructions which had hitherto dominated private urban building. Here the main stimulus was not only a concern to reduce the risk of fire but also a growing desire to emulate fashionable London, where building in brick had been made obligatory after the conflagration of 1666. At Warwick the new brick houses of the 1690s were designed to attract smart professional men into the town, while similar developments at about this time were probably responsible for Celia Fiennes's favourable comment on Nottingham: 'much like London'. Nonetheless, we must remember that most of these physical changes were still contained within the complex street pattern of the late medieval town: this was so even in the booming Restoration city of Bristol. Only in a few cases, like Northampton, were the town magistrates able to break away from the old ground-plan and design broad new streets more suitable for the new style of housing. And here, as in London, the catalyst was a great fire which destroyed much of the town in 1675.

How far urban building in the sixteenth and seventeenth centuries set the pace for the neighbouring countryside is not yet clear. We know from Burford that the advent of two-storey houses in the town was followed within fifty years by similar developments in adjoining villages. But overall it seems unlikely that the changing physical appearance of urban society after the Reformation had any extensive impact on the English countryside.

It was not only the town's physical image which lost its earlier power at the Reformation. From the later 1530s civic ceremonial came under attack. At Coventry, for example, the great processions of St. George's Day, Ascension, Whitsun, and Corpus Christi were all abolished by 1547; the Canterbury procession on the Eve of the Translation of St. Thomas had disappeared rather earlier. Mystery plays were similar victims of the new Protestant austerity; only a few, like those at Chester, lingered on until the end of the century as part of the entertainments for important visitors. No longer would civic pageants testify to the outside world the unity and pride of a particular town. The civic 'shows' which appeared in the later seventeenth century, the Godiva procession at Coventry, the Lord Mayor's inauguration at Norwich, and the town-sponsored horse-racing at Beverley and Lincoln, performed very different functions. They were primarily attempts to win the custom and patronage of county society by pandering to gentry taste.

So far as the religious role of the English town was concerned, the Reformation had a rather different effect. Certainly the Dissolution destroyed much of urban society's claim to provide the focal point of traditional Christianity, and, thereafter, apart from a brief recovery in Mary's reign, urban Catholicism steadily declined. By 1600, English Popery was a predominantly rural phenomenon. On the other hand, this did not mean that the religious influence of towns disappeared. Many now became leading propagators of the new Reformed truths. In London, Bristol, Canterbury, Gloucester, Sandwich, and possibly Exeter there were active groups of converts from the 1530s, helping in the demolition of the old order. It is true that in England towns never played the leading role in the Reform movement which they exercised in parts of the continent. There were no English equivalents to the cities of Nuremberg and Strasbourg, which championed the Protestant cause in Germany from the 1520s. One reason for this was the much weaker political position of English towns *vis à vis* the central government; another may have been the absence of that severe social and political tension which in some German cities seems to have provided a principal motor for religious change.

Nonetheless, by the early part of Elizabeth's reign urban Protestantism was undoubtedly an important force in English society. In the 1570s towns like Northampton and Bedford were centres of the prophesying movement and later in the reign they were frequently famous for the preaching power of their Puritan ministers, some of whom were appointed to special civic lectureships. One town preacher at Liverpool was so successful that the magistrates took pains to supplement his stipend by lending him 'a reasonable milk-cow, whilst he remains a preaching minister here'. Some towns ensured that their preachers gave their main sermons on market-days so as to reach the large number of countryfolk coming in to buy and sell.

Towns, moreover, were not content to serve merely as sounding-boards for the godly word. They also took the lead in enforcing the Puritan ethic, the suppression of gaming, vice and drunkenness, and the preservation of the sanctity of the English Sunday. Magisterial action along these lines was common from the 1580s onwards—well in advance of the statutory regulations of the Puritan Revolution. One such godly community was Nantwich where a later writer declared that great care was taken every year to elect churchwardens dedicated to putting down 'all disorders that trenched upon the Sabbath . . . [so that] there was scarce a market town within many miles where there was better order and more due observance of the Sabbath.' Urban Puritanism was the strongest expression of urban magistrates' interest in social control, faced as they were with the critical social problems described in earlier chapters. It was indeed a commonplace for Puritan preachers like Robert Jenison of Newcastle to declare that the problems which beset towns were evidence of deep-seated sins which must be rooted out of the community. Avarice and pride had brought upon them 'fearful fires, raging inundations, . . . plague and pestilence, and other judgements of scarcity, if not famine, of depopulation, or otherwise of denying a blessing to their labours and callings.'

By 1640, however, the role of towns as centres of radical Protestantism was losing much of its coherence. In the first place a number of towns, like Bristol, Norwich, and Canterbury, saw a growing split between moderate Puritans, committed to reforming the Church from within, and separatists who wanted a more sweeping programme of ecclesiastical reform. Though these divisions affected both town and countryside, the urban split was often aggravated by social tensions, with the separatists drawing their support from those small tradesmen and apprentices who felt angry at their exclusion from economic and civic power by moderate Puritan merchants. Another problem, at least in some areas, was the growing assumption of leadership within the godly cause by local gentlemen. More generally, the confidence of the Puritan élite was weakened by the Laudian attack on urban lectureships and godly magistrates during the 1630s. At Salisbury, for example, the trial in Star Chamber of the Puritan Recorder, Henry Sherfield, in 1633 demoralized the ruling élite, and at Gloucester there was a running battle between the conservative bishop, Godfrey Goodman, and the Puritan corporation, the latter desperately trying to retain their distinguished preacher, John Workman.

During the revolutionary era a number of towns sought to reassert their earlier primacy as strongholds of religious radicalism. In Salisbury, the themes of godly rule and Puritan social control evident in the 1620s were revived after 1646. The Gloucester magistrates took action against Laudian supporters, enforced a staunchly Puritan regime, and mounted a famous defence against Charles I's assault on the city in 1643. Richard Baxter noted the contrast between this town and Worcester, seeing in the former 'a civil, courteous and religious people, as different from those at Worcester as if they had lived under another government'. Further north, Manchester became the centre of the Presbyterian classis in South Lancashire. In general, however, towns failed to acquire a new religious importance during these decades. While the Fifth Monarchists were largely based in towns, the Ranters and Quakers drew their support mainly from the countryside.

After the Restoration the renewal of persecution led to some reforming of radical ranks. Despite the purge of nonconformist magistrates with the Corporation Act (1661), and the ban on dissenting ministers visiting towns under the Five Mile Act (1665), urban dissent remained active. Nonconformist groups were particularly powerful at Gloucester, Taunton, Dover, and Yarmouth. But urban evangelism now found little repsonse in the countryside, where the religious climate was markedly different from that prior to 1640. The gentry families, who increasingly controlled county government and rural society, regarded urban calls for religious reform as a certain prescription for renewed social disorder. They preferred to restore maypole dancing and those other folk games which urban radicals had helped to overthrow during the previous century. When the pressures on nonconformity were removed with the Toleration Act of 1689, urban Dissent remained active in the large centres. Bristol, for example, was a stronghold of the movement for Moral Reform in the 1690s, but the new staid respectability contrasted with the evangelical enthusiasm of earlier generations.

The educational function of urban society between 1500 and 1700 followed a similar fluctuating career. Despite the monastic and chantry connections of so many medieval schools, the majority of urban foundations managed to survive the religious upheavals of the 1530s and 1540s. Several became town grammar schools, as at Stratford, Ludlow, and Horsham. In addition, in the late sixteenth century, and to some extent in the early seventeenth, towns acquired a number of new secular foundations, many of them the work of London and provincial merchants, though a growing number of Puritan gentry were also involved in founding new schools. Professor W. K. Jordan has estimated that well over £293,000 was provided by benefactors in the years 1560–1640 'for the founding of schools in every quarter of the realm'. It would be wrong, however, to place exclusive emphasis on the role of endowed schools in educational expansion prior to 1640. In many towns they enjoyed only an exiguous life and taught a relatively small number of pupils. More influential were the numerous private, non-endowed schools which flourished from the Elizabethan period. Thus, at Faversham, the town grammar school (a monastic endowment refounded in the 1570s) had to share the educational market with five or six private schools at any one time. Most of these private establishments were so-called 'petty' or primary schools, teaching little more than reading and writing, but some at least provided secondary instruction.

This growth in urban schooling of all kinds was a response to two developments. The first was the spread of committed Protestantism among the middling ranks of urban society: this not only emphasized the spiritual importance of reading the Bible but the value of education in socializing the young child and orienting him towards the godly life. A no less important factor was the rapid growth of internal trade centred on towns, with the consequent demand for vocational literacy. Urban literacy rates probably rose sharply in the century or so before the Civil War. At Chester, for instance, as many as 58 per cent of adult male householders could sign their names in 1642; at Worcester a rather more select group of townsfolk showed a 65 per cent subscriptional literacy rate at the start of the seventeenth century. There was also a parallel increase in book-ownership during the period. In the 1590s, about 16 per cent of those Worcester men and women for whom probate inventories survive possessed one or more books, and in some of the Kentish towns the proportion was even higher.

Educational change was not confined to the towns but inevitably spilled over into the countryside. As well as attending those endowed schools which town merchants sometimes founded in villages, frequently their own places of birth, rural children often travelled into a neighbouring town for schooling. At the cathedral school in Worcester, for example, the majority of scholars probably came from outside the city; and even a town's petty schools attracted boys and girls from local villages, the children usually boarding with the teacher or with relations in town. In addition, urban centres helped to service the new educational skills of country people. By the early seventeenth century, Canterbury, for example, had an active group of booksellers selling a large quantity of books in East Kent, either directly to villagers who came to town, or indirectly through pedlars who retailed books in the villages.

Yet we must beware of exaggerating the contribution of education to the image and reputation of a particular town in the wider community. The suppression of the provincial printing presses in 1558 and the steady growth of government censorship in subsequent decades meant that almost all books, down to the simple school primer, came from officially approved printers in London. After 1600 the town was also becoming less important as a centre for schooling than it had been earlier. The growing class consciousness of the country gentry prompted an increasing number to withdraw their children from local, town grammar schools. They sent them instead to the great endowed schools like Westminster, Winchester, and Shrewsbury, to the rather expensive private schools now scattered across the countryside, and to the smart academies located in the London suburbs, like those of Mark Lewis at Tottenham and Thomas Singleton at Clerkenwell. Likewise peasant children were attracted to the growing number of rural petty schools; by 1640 almost 40 per cent of the country parishes in Canterbury diocese probably had a grammar or petty school, and most Cambridgeshire villages had a schoolmaster at some time or other between 1574 and 1628. Sometimes the reputation of a rural schoolmaster drew even the children of townsmen away from urban schools. The magistrates of Carlisle noted in the 1630s that in the past 'by reason of sedulous and painful schoolmasters, not only this city, but the whole country were partakers of the inestimable benefit that came thereby, for this seminary was like another Athens . . . ; but now we are glad, nay forward to send our children abroad into the country.' Competition from other establishments was not the only problem that faced endowed schools in seventeenth-century towns. Education was badly affected by the fragmentation of the old Puritan movement and the growth of civic corruption, with the frequent embezzlement of school lands and finances. After 1660 educational expansion ceased in most towns and established schools were often in dire straits. The school at Hull had virtually closed down by 1676 so that the townspeople were forced 'to send their children abroad to other schools in the country', and that at Coventry was said in 1685 to be 'in a sad, declining state, almost brought to nothing'. This stagnation of urban schooling was partially redressed at the end of the seventeenth century with the first appearance of charity schools. But they taught only simple literacy and confined almost all their energies to the children of the town.

In other areas the changing cultural function of the town is more difficult to chart. As we saw in chapter four, the seventeenth century witnessed the establishment of civic libraries in a number of major towns, but their cultural significance can easily be overstated. Most were small and they often lost their books almost as quickly as they acquired them; nor is there any evidence that they provided facilities for rural readers. The famous subscription libraries of the eighteenth century were still a world away. More strongly indicative of the prevailing level of urban culture was the absence outside London of any sustained interest in the urban past. Medieval mayoral annals rarely survive into the Stuart period and they were not replaced by works of urban antiquarianism comparable to the many surveys and histories of counties which appeared from the later sixteenth century onwards. There were only a handful of town histories, such as William Somner's *Antiquities of Canterbury* (1640), and Richard Butcher's *Survey and Antiquitie of the Towne of Stamford* (1646), and some of them remained unpublished until the nineteenth century. It is improbable that the revival of printing in larger towns like Bristol from the 1690s did much to resurrect cultural consciousness. Quite often these new provincial presses were run by agents or former servants of London printers.

In fact, by 1700 the social and cultural life of most provincial towns rarely had much civic inspiration. More often it was permeated by two, closely-related, outside influences. In the first place there was the powerful voice of county society. With the triumph of the country gentry after 1660, both in national and local politics, any town which recognized its own interests had to make the appropriate obeisance to county taste. Horse-racing, assembly rooms, theatres, and spas were all set up to attract the patronage of county gentry and to entertain those of them who were resident in the towns themselves. At Buckingham, for example, Henry Robinson built the Trolley House, a large assembly room in Castle Street, turned Castle Hill into a fashionable bowling green, and began a stage-coach service to London—all for the convenience and pleasure of the North Buckinghamshire gentry. Since by the end of our period the greater landowners were caught up in the machinations at Court and in the fashionable life of London, the new gentry involvement in urban affairs was confirmed by another outside influence, that of the metropolis. London-style fashions, London-style houses, London-style coffee and cocoa houses, all made an important impact on provincial towns in the later seventeenth century. Some of the larger towns like Norwich even had their own seasons, modelled on those of the metropolis, where less wealthy squires might take their ladies to be seen without the expense of a journey to London. Metropolitan influence was openly acknowledged in a Newcastle address to the rulers of the capital: 'Our eyes are on you; we . . . imitate your fashions, good or evil, and from you we fetch and frame our customs'.

By 1700, then, the old particularist image and influence of the English town, with its impressive cluster of public buildings and its wealth of civic, educational, and above all religious activity, had been heavily distorted, sometimes destroyed. In many places the urban community now functioned primarily as an adjunct to the social life of county society, exercising no distinctive role of its own. Even in the larger towns, which retained some cultural vitality in the later seventeenth century, the style and tone was set by the example of London. The closed civic commonwealths of the later Middle Ages, with their urban pride and individual local influence, had disappeared.

Conclusion

In the course of this book we have sought to describe and to explain the major changes affecting English towns in the sixteenth and seventeenth centuries. As we have often seen, towns varied widely in their local experience; even within the categories of town identified in the first five chapters, different communities often reacted in different ways to the more general developments which we have outlined in the second half of the book. Nevertheless, two broad themes may be discerned.

The first is the changing structure of the urban hierarchy itself between 1500 and 1700. The dominant position still held in 1500 by the medium-sized corporate towns, with their sophisticated political structure and distinctive cultural influence, was threatened during the sixteenth century by the rising prosperity of the simpler market-towns; and it was overthrown in the seventeenth century by the emergence of a smaller group of leading provincial centres, by the rapidly growing influence of the metropolis, and by the rise of new towns of a radically different kind from the old. This reshaping of the urban hierarchy dictated fundamental readjustments, especially for the county towns, throughout our period.

Our second, related, theme has been the external pressures imposed upon towns, affecting almost all their major functions. We have noticed the importance of national, demographic growth for urban populations, and of fluctuations in the levels of trade, prices, and migration for urban economic and social structures. We have also seen how national events like the Reformation and the Revolution affected the cultural and political life of towns. Until the middle of the seventeenth century these pressures were often critical, bringing the problems of declining industries and increasing poverty, of political conflict and social discontent, to the majority of

English towns. The stresses were not universal, nor were they constant, but it would be difficult to cite more than a handful of towns which did not suffer them for at least one or two generations in the century and a half before the Civil War.

In the second half of the seventeenth century, however, a new urban stability was starting to emerge. Some of the critical problems of the earlier period had subsided: pauper immigration seems to have declined; urban social structures may have been more stable; towns had found new economic roles or accepted the decay of old ones; corporations were beginning to adjust to political subservience and to welcome gentry interference for the economic gains which subsequently accrued. Above all, the reshaping of the urban hierarchy created a fresh equilibrium. There were important centres of economic growth in the new industrial towns; and other towns and ports which took advantage of the expansion of foreign trade did so without the hindrances of older civic forms of economic regulation which were now in decline. The dominance of London was fully established, and this had helped to create that integration and rationalization of the cultural, political, and economic life of the nation which was to bring significant benefits in the eighteenth century. But the new balance in the urban hierarchy was equally indicated by the prosperity of the provincial capitals—less rivals of the metropolis than mediators of its influence—and by the existence of new towns with specialist functions which London could not perform. By 1700 there was a more modern, open and integrated, urban society in England, compared with the traditional, relatively closed, and semi-autonomous worlds occupied by the corporate towns of the early sixteenth century.

However, if the benefits of hindsight present us with a favourable picture of urban society under the later Stuarts, our chapters have inevitably concentrated more heavily on the pressures and strains to which towns were earlier subjected. For these had dominated the consciousness of citizens and magistrates and determined the quality of urban life during the greater part of our period. The rulers of York articulated their own experience of urban transition when they coolly received Sir Thomas Widdrington's projected history of the town in 1660; and their remarks may fittingly conclude our own venture into urban history:

> 'You have told us . . . what the city was, and what our predecessors have been. We know not what this may have of honour in it: sure we are, it hath but little of comfort. The shoes of our predecessors are too big for our feet, and the ornaments which they had will not serve now to cover our nakedness. . . . Trade is decayed, the river become unnavigable . . . , Leeds is nearer the manufactures and Hull more commodious for the vending of them. . . . It is not a long series, or beadroll of ancestors and predecessors, but wealth and estate which set a value upon men and places.'

Map 1. The larger English towns c. 1520

Map 2. The larger English towns c. 1700

Select Bibliography

General

CHALKIN, C. W. *The Provincial Towns of Georgian England 1740–1820*, ch. i, (Arnold, London, 1974).

CLARK, PETER, (ed.). *The Early Modern Town: A Reader*, includes papers by Everitt, Rimmer, Minchinton, and Hoskins listed below, (Longman, London, 1976).

CLARK, PETER and SLACK, PAUL, (eds). *Crisis and Order in English Towns 1500–1700*, ch. i includes full bibliographical notes, (Routledge, London, 1972).

EVERITT, ALAN, (ed.). *Perspectives in English Urban History*, ch. i–iv, (Macmillan, London, 1973).

GROSS, CHARLES. *A Bibliography of British Municipal History*, 2nd edn., (Leicester U.P., Leicester, 1966).

HOSKINS, W. G. *Provincial England*, ch. iv–v, (Macmillan, London, 1963).

MARTIN, G. H. and MCINTYRE, S. *A Bibliography of British and Irish Municipal History: I*, excludes items in Gross, (Leicester U.P., Leicester, 1972).

Urban History Yearbook. An annual register of recent publications and research. (Leicester U.P., Leicester, 1974).

Chapter 1

BRAUDEL, F. *Capitalism and Material Life 1400–1800*, ch. viii, (Weidenfeld, London, 1973).

BREESE, GERALD, (ed.). *The City in Newly Developing Countries*, ch. xx, xxi, xxvi, xxix, (Prentice-Hall, Englewood Cliffs, 1969).

BRIDBURY, A. R. *Economic Growth: England in the later Middle Ages*, 2nd edn., (Harvester, Hassocks, 1975).

HAUSER, P. M. and SCHNORE, L. F., (eds.). *The Study of Urbanization*, ch. i, vii, xiii, xiv, (Wiley, New York, 1965).

JONES, EMRYS. *Towns and Cities*, (O.U.P., London, 1966).

PARK, R. E., BURGESS, E. W., and MCKENZIE, R. D. *The City*, 2nd edn., (Chicago U.P., Chicago, 1967).

SJOBERG, G. *The Preindustrial City: Past and Present*, (The Free Press, New York, 1960).

Victoria History of the Counties of England, especially the following volumes: *Oxfordshire*, X (Banbury); *Warwickshire*, VIII (Coventry and Warwick); *Wiltshire*, VI (Salisbury); and *Yorkshire: The City of York and East Riding*, I (Hull).

WEBER, MAX. *The City*, (The Free Press, New York, 1958).

WIRTH, L. 'Urbanism as a Way of Life', *American Journal of Sociology*, xliv, (1938).

Chapter 2

DYER, A. D. *The City of Worcester in the sixteenth century*, (Leicester U.P., Leicester, 1973).

EVERITT, ALAN. 'The Marketing of Agricultural Produce', ch. viii in *The Agrarian History of England and Wales: IV 1500–1640*, ed. J. Thirsk, (C.U.P., Cambridge, 1967).

Idem. 'The Banburys of England', *Urban History Yearbook: 1974*, (Leicester U.P., Leicester, 1974).

HILL, J. W. F. *Tudor and Stuart Lincoln*, (C.U.P., Cambridge, 1956).

PATTEN, JOHN. 'Village and Town: an Occupational Study', *Agricultural History Review*, xx, (1972).

RODGERS, H. B. 'The Market Area of Preston in the Sixteenth and Seventeenth Centuries', *Geographical Studies*, iii, (1956).

Chapter 3

BARTON, M. *Tunbridge Wells*, (Faber and Faber, London, 1937).

CHALKLIN, C. W. and HAVINDEN, M. A. (eds.). *Rural Change and Urban Growth 1500–1800*, ch. viii–x, (Longman, London, 1974).

COLEMAN, D. C. 'Naval Dockyards under the Later Stuarts', *Economic History Review*, 2nd series, vi, (1953–54).

COURT, W. H. B. *The Rise of the Midland Industries 1600–1838*, ch. iii–ix, (O.U.P., London, 1938).

GILL, C. *History of Birmingham, I*, (O.U.P., London, 1952).

RIMMER, W. G. 'The Evolution of Leeds to 1700', *Thoresby Society Publications*, L(2), (1967).

Chapter 4

Bristol Record Society, publications, especially vol. xii, xvii, xix, xxiv, xxv, xxvii–xxix.

BROCKETT, A. *Nonconformity in Exeter 1650–1875*, (Manchester U.P., Manchester, 1962).

HOSKINS, W. G. *Industry, Trade and People in Exeter 1688–1800*, 2nd edn., (Exeter U.P., Exeter, 1968).

HOWELL, ROGER. *Newcastle-upon-Tyne and the Puritan Revolution*, (Clarendon Press, Oxford, 1967).

MACCAFFREY, W. T. *Exeter 1540–1640*, 2nd edn., (Harvard U.P., Cambridge, Mass., 1976).

MINCHINTON, W. E. 'Bristol: Metropolis of the West in the Eighteenth Century', *Transactions of the Royal Historical Society*, 5th series, iv, (1954).

PALLISER, D. M. *The Reformation in York 1534–1553*, (Borthwick Paper, no. 40, St. Anthony's Press, York, 1971).

STEPHENS, W. B. *Seventeenth-Century Exeter*, (Exeter U.P., Exeter, 1958).

Chapter 5

BRENNER, R. 'The Civil War Politics of London's Merchant Community', *Past and Present*, no. 58, (1973).

BRETT-JAMES, N. G. *The Growth of Stuart London*, (Allen and Unwin, London, 1935).

DAVIS, RALPH. 'English Foreign Trade, 1660–1700', *Economic History Review*, 2nd series, vii, (1954).

FISHER, F. J. 'The Development of the London Food Market 1540–1640'. *Economic History Review*, 1st series, v(2), (1934–5).

Idem. 'The Development of London as a Centre of Conspicuous Consumption in the Sixteenth and Seventeenth Centuries', *Transactions of the Royal Historical Society*, 4th series, xxx, (1948).

Idem. 'London as an "Engine of Economic Growth" ', ch. i in *Britain and the Netherlands: IV*, eds. J. S. Bromley and E. H. Kossmann, (Nijhoff, The Hague, 1971).

GRASSBY, RICHARD. 'The Personal Wealth of the Business Community in Seventeenth-Century England', *Economic History Review*, 2nd series, xxiii, (1970).

JORDAN, W. K. *The Charities of London 1480–1660*, (Allen and Unwin, London, 1960).

LANG, R. G. 'London's Aldermen in Business: 1600–25', *Guildhall Miscellany*, iii, (1971).

PEARL, V. *London and the Outbreak of the Puritan Revolution*, (O.U.P., London, 1961).

RAMSAY, G. D. *The City of London in international politics at the accession of Elizabeth Tudor*, (Manchester U.P., Manchester, 1975).

REDDAWAY, T. F. *The Rebuilding of London after the Great Fire*, 2nd edn., (Arnold, London, 1951).

WRIGLEY, E. A. 'A Simple Model of London's Importance . . . 1650–1750', *Past and Present*, no. 37, (1967).

Chapter 6

GLASS, D. V. 'Two Papers on Gregory King', in *Population in History*, eds. D. V. Glass and D. E. C. Eversley, (Arnold, London, 1965).

HOLLINGSWORTH, M. F. and T. H. 'Plague Mortality Rates by Age and Sex in the Parish of St. Botolph's without Bishopsgate London, 1603', *Population Studies*, xxv, (1971).

JONES, P. E. and JUDGES, A. V. 'London Population in the late Seventeenth Century', *Economic History Review*, 1st series, vi, (1935).

PICKARD, R. *The Population and Epidemics of Exeter in Pre-Census Times*, (James Townsend, Exeter, 1947).

SHREWSBURY, J. F. D. *A History of Bubonic Plague in the British Isles*, (C.U.P., Cambridge, 1970).

SLACK, PAUL. 'Vagrants and Vagrancy in England 1598–1664', *Economic History Review*, 2nd series, xxvii, (1974).

WRIGLEY, E. A. *Population and History*, (Weidenfeld, London, 1969).

Chapter 7

GRASSBY, RICHARD. 'English Merchant Capitalism in the late Seventeenth Century', *Past and Present*, no. 46, (1970).

HOSKINS, W. G. 'The Elizabethan Merchants of Exeter', ch. vi in *Elizabethan Government and Society*, ed. S. T. Bindoff *et al.*, (Athlone Press, London, 1961).

KRAMER, STELLA. *The English Craft Gilds*, (Columbia U.P., New York, 1927).

MARSHALL, T. H. 'Capitalism and the Decline of the English Gilds', *Cambridge Historical Journal*, iii, (1929).

POUND, J. F. 'The Social and Trade Structure of Norwich 1525–1575', *Past and Present*, no. 34, (1966).

SUPPLE, B. E. *Commercial Crisis and Change in England 1600–1642*, ch. v, (C.U.P., Cambridge, 1959).

VANES, J., (ed.). *The Ledger of John Smythe 1538–1550*, (H.M.S.O., London, 1974).

Chapter 8

GLASS, D. V. 'Socio-economic Status and Occupations in the City of London at the end of the Seventeenth Century' in *Studies in London History*, eds. A. E. J. Hollaender and W. Kellaway, (Hodder and Stoughton, London, 1969).

JORDAN, W. K. *Philanthropy in England 1480–1660*, (Allen and Unwin, London, 1959).

POUND, J. F., (ed.). *The Norwich Census of the Poor 1570*, (Norfolk Record Society, xl, 1971).

SLACK, PAUL, (ed.). *Poverty in early Stuart Salisbury*, (Wiltshire Record Society, xxxi, 1976).

SMITH, S. R. 'Social and Geographical Origins of the London Apprentices 1630–60', *Guildhall Miscellany*, iv, (1971–3).

STONE, L. and EVERITT, A. 'Social Mobility', *Past and Present*, no. 33, (1966).

Chapter 9

CLARK, PETER. *English Provincial Society: Religion, Politics and Society in Kent 1500–1640*, ch. iv, xiii, (Harvester Press, Hassocks, 1976).

EVANS, J. T. 'The Decline of Oligarchy in Seventeenth-Century Norwich', *Journal of British Studies*, xiv, (1974).

GEORGE, R. H. 'The Charters Granted to English Parliamentary Corporations in 1688', *English Historical Review*, lv, (1940).

HIRST, D. *The Representative of the People? Voters and Voting in England under the Early Stuarts*, (Cambridge U.P., Cambridge, 1975).

NEALE, J. E. *The Elizabethan House of Commons*, ch. vii–xiii, (Cape, London, 1949).

PLUMB, J. H. 'The Growth of the Electorate in England from 1600 to 1715', *Past and Present*, no. 45, (1969).

SACRET, J. H. 'The Restoration Government and Municipal Corporations', *English Historical Review*, xlv, (1930).

WEBB, SIDNEY and BEATRICE. *The Manor and the Borough*, 2 vols., (Longman, London, 1908).

WEINBAUM, M. *The Incorporation of Boroughs*, (Manchester U.P., Manchester, 1937).

Chapter 10

BERGERON, D. M. *English Civic Pageantry*, (Arnold, London, 1971).

CLARK, PETER. 'The Ownership of Books in England 1560–1640: the Example of some Kentish Townsfolk', ch. iv in *Schooling and Society*, ed. L. Stone, (Johns Hopkins U.P., Baltimore, 1976).

CRANFIELD, G. A. *The Development of the Provincial Newspaper 1700–1760*, (Clarendon Press, Oxford, 1962).

PORTMAN, D. *Exeter Houses 1400–1700*, (Exeter U.P., Exeter, 1966).

SEAVER, P. S. *The Puritan Lectureships*, (Stanford U.P., Stanford, 1970).

SIMON, B., (ed.). *Education in Leicestershire 1540 to 1940*, ch. i–ii, (Leicester U.P., Leicester, 1968).

STONE, L. 'The Educational Revolution 1560–1640', *Past and Present*, no. 28, (1964).

Index

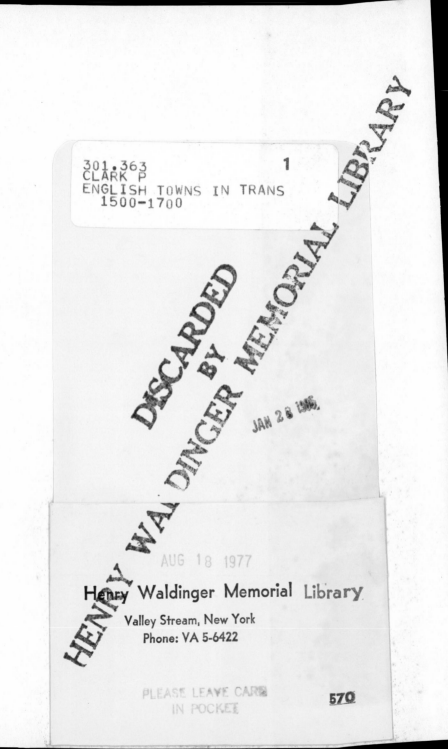